CHERYL AND ASHLEY
LOVE WARS

CHERYL AND ASHLEY
LOVE WARS

JOHN MCSHANE

JOHN BLAKE

Published by John Blake Publishing Ltd,
3 Bramber Court, 2 Bramber Road,
London W14 9PB, England

www.johnblakepublishing.co.uk

First published in paperback in 2010

ISBN: 978 1 84358 195 6

British Library Cataloguing-in-Publication Data:

A catalogue record for this book is available from the British Library.

Design by www.envydesign.co.uk

Printed in Great Britain by Bookmarque Ltd, Croydon CR0 4TD

1 3 5 7 9 10 8 6 4 2

Papers used by John Blake Publishing are natural, recyclable products
made from wood grown in sustainable forests. The manufacturing processes
conform to the environmental regulations of the country of origin.

CONTENTS

1

EARLY YEARS

Cheryl Tweedy and Ashley Cole had a lot in common. They were young, they were rich and they were famous. There was also another factor that united the pair. Both were born, as the Americans would say, 'on the wrong side of the tracks'.

Cheryl came from Newcastle, as working-class a city as one can imagine; Ashley was an East End boy from London. Neither of them starved or experienced poverty in childhood – their stories weren't Dickensian in that sense – but there were no silver spoons in sight, either.

Yet, by the time they were barely out of their teens, they had both started to conquer their respective worlds due to a mixture of natural ability, hard work and the determination to succeed. Their stories seemed too good to be true – or should that be too good to last?

Cheryl's began on 30 June 1983, when she was born in

Newcastle General Hospital. Her mother Joan already had two sons and a daughter, and another brother, Garry, would be born four years later. Cheryl's father was a local painter and decorator, Garry Tweedy. The family lived in a terraced council house in Cresswell Street, Walker, an area that Cheryl later admitted was 'very tough'.

Even as a baby and then a toddler, Cheryl had striking dark good looks. Everyone noticed them and commented on how pretty she was. Her mother was urged to enter her for contests, and little Cheryl won one sponsored by Boots, the chemist chain, and another run by Mothercare. She also won a Little Miss and Mister contest organised by the local newspaper, the *Evening Chronicle*.

Her mother took her to an agency and soon little Cheryl had an impressive portfolio of work as a child model. She was filmed in the bath for a British Gas commercial showing how much fun it was to have gas supplied into the home and in May 1990 she took part in the National Garden Festival at Gateshead. She was on her way.

The same year she won £150 of clothing vouchers when she came first in the 'Star of the Future' contest, again organised by the Newcastle newspaper. Never can a local 'rag' have run a competition with such an apt title.

'My dad supported all of us because my mum wanted to bring us up,' she was to recall. 'There wasn't a lot of money, but Mum and Dad always found enough for my audition outfits. I was the little show-off in the family.'

She added, 'We didn't have any privileges. I remember living on baked beans, eggs and bread – if it wasn't out of date. If we got a McDonald's or a Chinese takeaway – oh my God, that was a treat, a luxury, because it was costing my mother a fortune.

'I'd get a Barbie that was four years out of fashion from a girl in the street who didn't want it any more. And I'd get hand-me-downs from a girl up the road who had everything she wanted. Then she'd be, like, 'Ha ha! Cheryl's got my jumper on!'

Cheryl also took dancing lessons and from the age of six would enter stage contests in and around Newcastle.

When she was ten she was chosen to attend the Summer School of the Royal Ballet at Richmond Park in London but hated it. She said, 'I wanted to go home straightaway. Everyone was prim and proper and I was just a Geordie from a council estate. Their parents all had money and we struggled just to get the money to travel down to London. I felt that I was the odd one out.'

After training for a fortnight and crying every evening because of homesickness, she performed a routine for a panel of judges. But she said, 'I was the only one waving to my mum, excited to see her.' She decided she did not want to be a dancer, pointing out, 'It shattered my dream but I didn't want to have to stand a certain way all my life and only eat salad.'

Much more to her liking was the First Act Theatre group back in Newcastle, which provided training in all aspects of theatre and stage life for youngsters. And, by the start of 1994, she appeared on stage for the first time and performed a dance solo at the Whitley Bay Playhouse in

Aladdin, and a year later, with a boy partner, took part in the UK National Dance Championships in Blackpool.

Soon Cheryl, whose parents separated when she was 11, was singing as well as dancing, but she also had to earn a living, and, after leaving school, worked for a spell as a waitress at a café near her home before the big break came.

Cheryl was accepted for an audition for *Popstars: The Rivals* at Wembley in August 2002 and she wowed the judges. Peter Waterman said of her, 'You would need to be dead if you didn't think she was stunning. My God!' And Louis Walsh's verdict was, 'You have the most beautiful eyes and skin I have ever seen in my life.'

Cheryl's success in the show led to happy scenes in Newcastle, although her sister Gillian and elder brother Andrew – of whom we will hear more later – were both arrested after a celebration ended in a brawl and were subsequently bound over to keep the peace.

But nothing could apparently mar the success that was now to come Cheryl's way as she joined the girl band that resulted from the show. Girls Aloud were born and instantly had a Christmas Number One, 'Sound of the Underground'. It was a quick taste of what lay ahead for the five girls, who many thought would disappear quietly from view but who went on to stardom instead.

Unfortunately, there was trouble waiting around the corner in January 2003 in the shape of a violent incident at a nightclub in Guildford that could have had a disastrous effect on Cheryl's career. It resulted in her spending the night in a police cell and being charged two months later after she was accused of punching nightclub toilet attendant Sophie Amogbokpa, 39, in the face and calling her a 'f***ing black bitch'.

When the case was eventually dealt with in October 2003, a judge called Cheryl's behaviour an 'unpleasant piece of drunken violence'. She was found guilty of assault but cleared of yelling racist insults and she buried her head in her hands as the verdict was delivered by the jury. She escaped jail, however, and was sentenced to 120 hours' community service.

Judge Richard Haworth told her at the end of the eight-day trial at Kingston Crown Court, 'This was an unpleasant piece of drunken violence which caused Sophie Amogbokpa pain and suffering. Her eye was painful for three or four weeks, there was bruising for three months, and for a while she had blurred vision. You showed no remorse whatsoever.'

The jury had heard evidence that Cheryl came out of a loo cubicle 'completely paralytic' and went berserk when asked to pay for some lollipops near the attendant. Cheryl was eventually found guilty by an 11–1 majority verdict of the lesser assault charge – assault causing actual bodily harm – after the jury of seven men and five women failed to reach a unanimous decision after deliberating for nearly three hours.

Afterwards, Cheryl issued a statement saying, 'I'm pleased that the trial is over and thankful that the jury has accepted that this incident has nothing to do with race. I am not a racist and anyone who knows me knows I would not say anything racist. I'm stunned and disappointed by the conviction for assault. I would like to thank my family, friends and fans for their support.'

Cheryl said she acted in self-defence and the attendant threw the first punch. Her defence argued that nightclub staff made up the racial element of the attack to sell their story to a newspaper.

Later, Cheryl was to explain, 'The worst thing for me at the time was being called a racist. Anyone who knows me knows that's so far from the truth and I find it insulting. It's just horrible. The only thing worse I can think of is to be called a prostitute.

'The kind of guys I go for are mixed-race, and I have ex-boyfriends who are mixed-race who were prepared to stand up for me in court.

'The whole trial experience was traumatic. In the courtroom I was going through all sorts of scenarios in my head. I just didn't know what to think. I tried not to think about going to prison because in my heart I knew what had and hadn't happened.

'I just held onto that glimmer of hope that people would believe me. I lost seven or eight pounds during the trial. I couldn't eat a thing. I'd put something in my mouth but I just couldn't swallow it; it was horrible.

'My mum moved down to be with me for a week before the case. I just wanted her there with me – I couldn't have coped without her. She was my rock. I was totally useless, I couldn't do anything for myself and I was in tears all the time. She washed and ironed all my clothes and cleaned my flat.

'The whole family wanted to come to court to support me, but I had to say no because it would have been a media circus. I feel awful for putting them through all this, but they were fantastic.'

Although she was cleared of racially aggravated assault, there was no doubt that the court proceedings had been an ordeal for Cheryl. It is a tribute to both her character and her determination that she was able to put it behind her and concentrate on her future with Girls Aloud, which was soon to go from success to success.

What of Ashley Cole while this was going on?

The young defender (he was born on 20 December 1980) was already first choice left-back for Arsenal and England and had appeared for the national side in the 2002 World Cup finals, but, as with Cheryl's career, it had not been an easy route to the top.

His mother, too, was a strong figure in his life, and, like his bride-to-be, he grew up in an environment that could easily have led him astray. There are remarkable similarities in their upbringing, which emerged when Ashley gave an insight into his background and what drove him on in several interviews with journalists eager to talk to one of the most exciting talents to have emerged in years, when he first burst on the scene with Arsenal.

'I grew up in Stepney, east London, and my background was far from privileged,' he said. 'But my mum got me whatever I wanted, or tried to get me whatever I wanted, because she wanted the best for me.

'My mum brought us up – me and my younger brother Matthew – without my dad. She worked as a helper at my primary school. We were never spoiled but she would always fork out for new trainers and smart clothes. She couldn't drive but she never missed a single game of football I played.

'We've never really spoken about it, but bringing up two kids on her own must have been a real struggle. We lived in a two-bedroom council flat, so my brother and I had to share a room.

'There was a lot of crime in the area but luckily I was into football, so I stayed out of trouble. I wasn't the brainiest kid in the school and always sat at the back, but I was a good student and went every day – my mum made me.

'Outside school, I was always down the park kicking a football and rolling around in the mud. David Rocastle, Alan Smith and Ian Wright [all Arsenal players] were my idols.

'Then, when I was six or seven, my mum and Uncle Teddy took me to our local Sunday team, Puma. Then I got picked for my district and Arsenal, and the rest is history.

'I started training at Highbury after school, and in my school holidays we used to play matches at the training ground. There was never any chance of me joining another club. My heart was at Arsenal; I just wanted to play for them.'

In those days he was a striker: 'I played upfront for my Sunday league team, but when I was at Arsenal as a schoolboy I got put on the left wing. Then one day the youth team, a year older than me, didn't have a left-back. I was still a schoolboy, just 15, and the others were YTS [Youth Training Scheme] trainees, and it was good for me to get put up a year. I must have done OK because I've stayed at left-back ever since. It's strange, but everybody I know in the pro game had ended up in a different position to the one they played as a schoolboy.

'I'll never forget meeting Ian Wright because he was so loud. As soon as we walked into training he would be laughing and making jokes. He was the man – I wanted to be like him.'

In later years Ashley would become known for his love of flash cars and would alternate between driving his Lamborghini and his Bentley – but in the early days back in May 2001 it was different.

'At the moment I still drive around in my little Renault Clio,' he said then, 'but I'm getting a black convertible Audi TT at the end of the season and I'm moving into a new flat in a nice part of London.

'I get most pleasure buying things for my mum. She doesn't really like it but I get her shoes, clothes, anything she wants. She's done everything for me in the past and it's my way of repaying her.'

He added, 'I was at home with mum and my brother phoned and said, "Look at the telly – you're in the England squad."

'I couldn't believe it when I saw my name there – I was so scared I thought, "Do I have to go through this?" Mum just said she was proud of me. Playing for England is everything you dream about.'

By the end of the 2003–4 Premiership season, Ashley was no longer a new kid on the block, nor was he driving around in old cars. By that summer he was a member of the all-conquering Arsenal side and one of the national side's star players – his 'dream' had come true.

He and Cheryl had both made it, in spite of the odds, in their respective careers, and the glittering prizes were ahead of them. They had both achieved so much so rapidly, but they had not yet met. That was soon to happen, with remarkable consequences.

2

SPARKS

Where did the paths of Ashley Cole and Cheryl Tweedy first cross? Where was the romantic, glamorous spot on the jet-setters' map of the world where the successful young footballer and the beautiful pop singer met for the first time and began the love affair that was to fascinate millions? It was in, of all places, a psychiatric hospital or, to be more accurate, a *former* psychiatric hospital that had, some years earlier, been converted into a massive complex of luxury apartments.

The foundation stone for the Middlesex County Pauper Lunatic Asylum at Colney Hatch in Friern Barnet, north London, had been laid by Prince Albert in 1850 and the hospital took in its first patients on 17 July 1851, the year Queen Victoria opened the Great Exhibition at Crystal Palace.

When it took in its first patients it was the largest asylum in Europe, with six miles of corridors and a frontage nearly 1,884 feet long. The asylum, which occupied a massive 14 acres, was built for 1,000 patients, many of whom helped with the cooking and the cleaning; but, as the population of London and its surrounding suburbs grew, the asylum became overcrowded. Extensions were built between 1857 and 1859, so that 2,000 patients could be housed. By the 1860s the hospital staff were unable to cope with all the new inmates, and they had to resort to extreme measures to control many of them, frequently using straitjackets and other methods of restraint for those who were difficult to control.

In the 1880s conditions at Colney Hatch, together with the general fear and prejudice against mental disorders, had made the asylum unpopular with local people. Indeed the words 'Colney Hatch' became synonymous with the mentally ill, just as 'Bedlam' – derived from the Bethlem Royal Hospital – has.

During the 1890s the hospital built a number of wooden huts to house even more patients, and by 1898 there were 2,500. Early in 1903 three of these huts caught fire and 51 patients were killed. It was the worst fire in a hospital ever known in Britain, and so, in 1908, the huts were replaced with proper brick buildings, meaning it took a visitor over five hours to walk around its wards, so massive was the hospital, which, at its peak, housed 3,500 patients. Those were the days when anywhere that cared for the mentally ill was dubbed a 'loony bin', and the building fitted that coarse description to a T.

Among those who heard the heavy doors shut behind them were John Duffy, a serial killer and mass rapist, Aaron Kosminski, one of the leading Jack the Ripper suspects and Dorothy Lawrence, a woman who dressed as a man in order to fight on the front lines in World War One and was to spend the last 40 years of her life in mental institutions.

There were several name changes in the hospital's history before, in 1993, it closed for the final time, only to be reborn in the property boom years as Princess Park Manor, one the most desirable housing developments in the area.

It boasted, 'The Italianate splendours of Princess Park Manor provide a luxury living link with the glory of Victorian England', and, in case the message hadn't got across, it was also described by the company who sold homes there as 'A Victorian masterpiece which has delighted and inspired aficionados of fine architecture for generations'. No mention, understandably perhaps, of straitjackets, fire deaths, Jack the Ripper or serial killers.

It was home to a state-of-the-art health-and-fitness club with a 20-metre swimming pool, a superbly equipped gym, a restaurant and bar.

By the time that Ashley and Cheryl were dominating headlines around the world, the largest home at Princess Park Manor was on the market at just under £2 million; an 'ordinary' three-bedroom apartment wouldn't leave much change out of £1 million. And Princess Park Manor could also proudly lay claim to having tennis courts for its well-heeled residents to keep trim on.

It was on one of those courts that Ashley met Cheryl and the saga of their strife-torn love began on a hot summer's day in August 2004. Both lived in apartments at Princess Park Manor, coincidentally on the same floor, and he had previously seen her walking past when he had visited his friend and former Arsenal colleague, Paolo Vernazza

Cheryl walked past the window of Vernazza's ground-floor apartment and Ashley spotted her. She was to recall his first attempt at attraction her attention: 'I walked past the window and he shouted: "Hey, hot lips!" and "Nice bum."

'I hate stuff like that, so I rolled my eyes and was, like, "Piss off!" But the more I saw him in the papers the more I couldn't stop thinking about him.'

By his own admission Ashley used to 'sprint to the window' to look at Cheryl, having already, like the rest of the nation, seen her pictures in newspapers and magazines; but, apart from that, their paths did not cross. Not until that fateful day on the tennis courts, that is.

Ashley's opponent was Jermaine Pennant, another teammate at Arsenal. At the time, Pennant held the record for being the youngest player to appear in Arsenal's first team at 16 years, 319 days. Although that milestone has since been broken, by the talented Spaniard Cesc Fàbregas, Pennant is also in the record books for another achievement: becoming the first professional footballer to play a match wearing an electronic tag, while on probation for a drink-driving conviction.

Pennant was to play a key role in the meeting between Ashley and Cheryl, as he had already met her bandmate

Kimberley Walsh. She was with Cheryl that day, and so Pennant had an excuse to call them over for a chat. Perhaps Ashley and Cheryl would have met one way or another, no matter, but who can say what would have happened if Ashley had had another tennis opponent that day and Pennant hadn't been there to act as a catalyst for their meeting?

As it was, 'Penno' saw the girls driving away from the apartments. They were on their way that stifling hot day to buy an electric cooling fan, and they stopped their car and came over to talk to the footballers.

It was hot, unusually so for an English summer, and Ashley was sweating profusely. Perhaps it was just the heat, perhaps it was also the effect that Cheryl was having on him as they chatted and laughed together through the netting surrounding the tennis court. He would later say, 'I had this weird sense she was right for me. Here was someone on my wavelength. I knew it there and then. Can't explain it. Just knew it.'

It would be hard to put it any more clearly than that.

The girls went out on their shopping trip, and when they returned Cheryl discovered that Ashley was having problems with his Aston Martin. It had a flat battery and, through the wound-down window of her car, they picked up where they had left off with their small talk. Eventually, Ashley, who always felt he was basically a shy person when it came to talking to the girls, summoned up the courage to ask Cheryl for her number. She wouldn't give it to him.

The next time the two met, again near their apartments, she said she had felt ill at ease at their earlier meeting because she felt her hair was a mess, there was no makeup on her face and, in short, she looked terrible.

Ashley, on the other hand, had just appeared in a photoshoot for *Zoo* magazine, one of the leading lads' mags, in which he had looked mean, moody and magnificent. She couldn't resist a quip about the pictures: 'See yourself in the magazine. Looking good!' He wasn't sure if she was being flattering or the remark was made with her tongue firmly in her Geordie cheek.

One thing was for sure, however: contact had been well and truly made. Whether it would go any further than that was still in the balance until Cheryl went back home to Newcastle. At the age of 17 she had been to have her fortune read by 41-year-old clairvoyant Gareth Francis from the Spital Tongues region of the city.

Four years on, she decided to accompany her mother and go and see him again. Amazingly he told her that she knew a footballer and had read about him in a magazine. Not only that, but she would be married by the time she was 24!

So impressed has Cheryl been with psychic Francis that she encouraged the former hotel receptionist to persevere with writing his first book, aimed at children, called *Witches in Stitches*, about friends who discover their teachers are spooks in disguise.

Later she said, 'I actually fancied Ashley but had decided not to do anything about it because of what he had shouted at me. But Gareth said, "You need to pursue this, it's great." So he gave me the push to give Ashley my number.'

But it would have been a little too obvious for her to make contact directly with Ashley, even though they lived moments from each other. So Kimberley texted Cheryl's number to Pennant and he passed it to the England full-back. Mission accomplished.

Armed with that all-important number, Ashley could now make the next move. It is at this point that the phrase 'and he wasted no time' should appear, but Ashley wasn't going to play it like that. He waited an entire week before responding, but even then he did it very gently.

He decided to send her a text in order to elicit a response. That in itself would have been a tentative way of going about things, but he chose to send it at 1am, thinking that, at that time of the morning, her phone would be switched off. Some might call it, unfairly, the coward's way of dating. If Ashley thought this was a low-key way of doing things, he had picked the wrong night.

Cheryl and the rest of Girls Aloud were on tour and they were in Scotland that night. They'd just finished a show and the adrenalin was still pumping. Cheryl was very wide awake as she responded to her phone and the question Ashley was posing: 'Fancy meeting up?' She wasted no time in replying, and for the next 20 minutes the texts passed back and forth between the two of them, their fingers working furiously as they sent messages to each other. And, yes, she did fancy meeting up.

Both were high-profile, both were instantly recognisable,

so the question of where to go for that first date was a difficult one. In any of the usual celeb haunts, they would be spotted straightaway, the cat would be out of the bag and there would be no real chance to get to know each other. This was where they had that stroke of luck in both living in the same building. There were no paparazzi walking around the corridors of Princess Park Manor, no camera lenses pointed at the windows inside its gated, security-guarded grounds. Better still, there would be no eager journalists or people ready to tip off the newspapers with news of the fledgling romance in the hope of being paid for their indiscretion. So what better place than Ashley's apartment for that all-important first date and, as Ashley described, it 'a bite to eat and a few drinks'?

After that there was no stopping their romance. They saw each other daily, unless his football commitments and her work with the band got in the way of their meeting. Understandably, they were both cautious about the way their romance would progress, as Cheryl later explained: 'We'd both recently come out of relationships and we wanted to start out as friends and get to know each other. But we got to the point where I thought, "I just don't want to meet someone else." I was kidding myself by playing it cool, so I said to him one day, "I don't want us to see other people." '

Then, one night, as they watched television at Ashley's apartment, he said he loved her. 'I was making him laugh, pulling funny faces and doing silly voices. You know when you say something before your brain's even thought about it. His face went green, it dropped a mile. He looked scared. I was pissing myself laughing, howling. Then later I texted him to say I loved him too.'

Secretive as they quite understandably were, it was only a matter of time before the world would know of their love, and it was somehow fitting where that revelation took place.

Funky Buddha is an achingly trendy members-only nightclub in Mayfair – and one that was to feature again in the story of Ashley and Cheryl – and it was there that they were first seen as an item.

Soon, brief stories appeared in two gossip columns in the tabloids, referred to, somewhat sneeringly, as the 'red-tops'. One said, 'We stumbled upon Girls Aloud babe Cheryl Tweedy, 20, enjoying an intimate chat with Arsenal and England star Ashley Cole, 23. Later the Geordie babe took to the floor for a bit of a dirty dance with the strapping lad.'

Another reported, 'Cheryl Tweedy made a beeline for Arsenal ace Ashley Cole – and within minutes they were dancing cheek to cheek. She insists they are just friends. But an onlooker said: "They were slow dancing and looked very much like a couple."'

If these were veiled references to the couple's closeness, there could be no doubt about what was being said when, the next day, 29 October, the *Sun*, in its 'Bizarre' column, edited by Victoria Newton – under a headline that couldn't resist a pun: CHERYL IS ASHLEY'S GOALFRIEND – the following appeared: 'Gorgeous Cheryl Tweedy is dating Arsenal ace

Ashley Cole, I can reveal ... England defender Ashley, who split up with his long-term girlfriend Emily in July, is said to be "very keen" on Geordie Cheryl.

A pal of Ashley's said: "He really likes Cheryl and thinks she's lovely" ...' The paper added, '[Cheryl] previously dated Newcastle wildman Kieron Dyer. Less enviably, fellow Geordie Gazza (or G8 as he now likes to be known) has also revealed he has a crush on her ... Cheryl is often voted the sexiest one in the band and is a firm favourite with most lads' mags.'

Another newspaper quoted Cheryl as saying she was 'smitten' with Ashley. It's a lovely, old-fashioned way of verbally expressing affection for someone, deriving as it does from the verb 'to smite'. If only Cheryl had known that one definition of the word is 'to inflict serious defeat on'. Perhaps she might, with the benefit of hindsight, have phrased her feelings differently.

It seemed a marriage, or at least a partnership, made in heaven: the handsome young footballer with the world and a ball at his feet and the beautiful young singer, poised on the brink of stardom that even *she* probably did not anticipate at that stage. They had both come from modest backgrounds to achieve their fame and success. Surely it was the perfect match.

However, what the newspapers did not mention, no doubt because they were unaware of it at the time, was that, later that evening, Ashley moved his attention to another beautiful young woman at the club. Minutes after saying goodbye to Cheryl, who had work commitments the next day, he approached Alexandra Taylor in the nightclub bar after eyeing her up from the VIP area.

Eventually the beauty therapist, then 22, from Blackpool, left the club separately from Ashley but, as they had arranged, was reunited with him at his flat. There, as she was one day to tell the world, they made love, albeit somewhat speedily and slightly disappointingly.

That night, and how Ashley behaved during the course of it and with the Lancashire lass he met, is something that we will return to later in detail. But it wasn't the one and only time he and Alexandra were together, because, for the next two months, they saw each other frequently at nightclubs that were popular with both models and footballers.

Although they never made love again, they would kiss, cuddle and be affectionate with each other. And all the time, as far as the public and the outside world knew, he was dating Cheryl.

It is important to remember that, in spite of their celebrity status, both Ashley and Cheryl were still very young: he was 23 and she was 21. But fame is a harsh master, and there was to be no escaping the almost microscopic analysis that their relationship would now come under. They had enjoyed that brief, sweet, two-month period between their initial conversation at a sunlit tennis court and the darkness of a neon-lit nightclub in early winter, a period in which they could develop as a couple away from the spotlight. That had now ended, and their subsequent time together was to be analysed by the media and the public in a manner that could be described as 'merciless' at best and 'obsessive' at worst. For better or worse 'The Ashley–Cheryl' show had begun.

Many of the reports of their time together were to be misinformed, and two incorrect ones set the trend pretty quickly. One said that Ashley had decided to buy an apartment at Princess Park Manor to be near her. This either ignored the fact that he already lived there or was written without knowledge of that fact.

Another was headlined, CHERYL IN LOVE SPLIT – a grim prophecy of what was to come, perhaps, but totally wrong at the time. Perhaps it was in reaction to that report that, a couple of days later, Cheryl became the first of the couple to talk openly of their feelings for each other.

'Things are really good between us. He makes me very happy and puts a big smile on my face.' By the time she made these remarks at the end of November 2004, Ashley had taken the step that so many had taken before – meeting the girlfriend's mum.

Joan had come down to London the previous week and stayed at the flat in Friern Barnet that Cheryl shared with her bandmate Nicola Roberts. 'My mam really approves of him,' Cheryl said at the time.

At that stage in the relationship, Ashley had managed to refrain from splashing out on anything untoward for his girlfriend. 'He hasn't bought any presents for me,' Cheryl had to admit, although she took a different view of his forthcoming 24th birthday on 20 December. 'I'm not going to tell you what I'm plotting but let's just say he won't be disappointed,' she said.

It was not going to be a quiet run-in to that birthday party – how could it be, given the nature of the life that both Ashley and Cheryl were now living?

One of the burdens of fame in modern society is that there is the ever-present possibility – or perhaps that should be probability – that an old flame will appear and come forth with revelations about earlier behaviour that range from the indiscrete to the downright embarrassing. Both Ashley and Cheryl were to suffer from this modern-day curse, and Ashley was first in the firing line.

Care worker Emma Barrett, 24, who spent five years with Ashley as he rose from soccer apprentice to England ace, accused him of cheating on her and lying to her over his behaviour in an interview that she gave to the tabloid Sunday paper the *People*.

She didn't pull any punches either: 'I can't believe how much Ashley's changed. He's like a rat, a little rodent all over the place.

'Cheryl is going to have her work cut out if she thinks she can tame him because she is a pop star. He will cheat on her again and again like he did with me.'

Emma, who grew up near Ashley in east London said, 'He's changed from someone who cared about people to a Mr Hot Shot who thinks because he kicks a football around he doesn't need to care about anyone else. I loved him once but not any more.'

Emma, who began dating Ashley when he was a £30-a-week apprentice cleaning boots at Arsenal, recalled the first time they made love. She said, 'He was shy and nervous. It was the first time we'd spent the night together and neither of us really knew what we were doing.

'He used to be quite embarrassed when he got out of bed in the morning and draped the duvet round him. He was much better with balls on the pitch.

'The best way to sum it up is a match lasts 90 minutes but Ash was more like 90 seconds in bed.

'You read about footballers being told not to have sex to save energy. If that's true, Ash should be the fittest England player in the team.'

According to the *People*, Emma was to suffer the heartache that would haunt Cheryl years later, when, in 2002, newspapers named two women Ashley had passionate flings with. He denied both, but Emma said, 'I found out that, although he was my Ash, the soccer star Ashley Cole had been dating these models. I began to hear about him with other girls. I'd say to him, "Ash, I heard this" and he would say, "Em, don't take no notice. People think they know stuff – they are lying to you." And I didn't believe it to start with.'

That year Ashley was picked for the England squad for the World Cup in Japan.

'He asked me to go but I couldn't. I was working helping disabled children at a local school. I don't even like football. I let him go do his thing. However, I caught him out. While he was there he had left his old phone with his mum. I went through it and found a girl called Sophie's number in it. I phoned him about it and he said, "I don't know who she is." So I rang her up and she described the inside of his house. When he returned, I took her round there. He was saying "Who is this girl? I've never seen here, who are you?" But she was pointing out where everything was – she had obviously been there before. He just couldn't help lying,' she told the paper.

After five years together the couple split. She said, 'It was at the point where he was saying, "I can't see you tonight" and I didn't believe the reasons. The next time we saw each other was at a club in Enfield. We had words and one of my friends stepped in to say calm down.'

Emma always got on well with Ashley's mum Sue, who organised a girls' break to the Dominican Republic the previous year. Emma said, 'I couldn't go because of school term time. His mum said Ash would pay my wages if I left my job until I found a new one so I could come on holiday. So I left my job.' Emma had subsequently been with Sue to New York and Spain.

Emma said that payments Ashley had been making to her stopped and she repeatedly telephoned to discuss the matter with him. Cheryl, feeling that Ashley was being pestered, spoke to her.

Emma said, 'I can understand why she was upset but I was still very shocked by her reaction and the way she spoke to me. She screamed "What are you doing ******* phoning my ******* boy-friend?" Then she called me a "slag", so I asked to speak to Ash and he said he stopped the money ages ago. He was lying, so I hung up,' the *People* reported.

Emma added, 'He is a different person now. It's depressing the way he has changed because of all this hero-worship. Good luck to him and Cheryl. They deserve each other.'

The report concluded with Ashley's solicitor, Graham Shear, who said, 'We do not wish to dignify these allegations and inaccuracies with any comment.' And Cheryl's spokesman said the singer had not spoken to Emma.

It was not the first time that there had been a kiss-and-tell about Ashley, nor was it to be the last.

Whatever the truth of the matter and who said what to whom, it was hardly the type of story either Ashley or Cheryl needed; nor was the item in the '3am' column in the *Daily Mirror*, the paper's showbiz-led gossip page, which said the birthday party did not go as planned, as no sooner had Cheryl arrived than she was to storm out 30 minutes later in floods of tears'.

An onlooker told the paper that Ashley looked 'absolutely gutted' when she left. It had all started so well and Cheryl was all smiles as she arrived at the bash, held at the swanky London club Tantra. '[The onlooker said] "One of Ash's mates made a comment about Cheryl and she took it really badly. She started laying into Ash's pal and that sparked the argument. She'd only been at the party for five minutes – they'd had a kiss and were holding hands. But things just turned nasty. After a bit of a barney Cheryl stormed off and we thought that was going to be the end of it. Everyone hoped she'd calm down and would be OK. But unfortunately the argument kicked off again about half an hour later and it was much worse. Cheryl was in tears. She was laying into Ash. And Nicola was telling him: 'Cheryl's furious. And if someone said something nasty about me, I would be too.'"'

A friend of the pair told the paper, 'It ruined the night for both of them. Cheryl thinks he acts differently when his pals are around. When they're alone he's the sweetest guy in the world but when his mates are there he's really distant. He spent half the night talking into his mobile – that hacked her off a lot.'

Hours after that reported bust-up – Ashley actually said later that it was 'rubbish' to say there had been a row – Cheryl jetted back home to Newcastle and was spotted shopping in the city's Eldon Square area.

While Cheryl had let slip just enough about their relationship to confirm it was 'on' – prior to the misunderstanding in the nightclub – it was Ashley's turn next to have his say. Despite being reported to have spent £4,000 on a watch for her, he said, 'We didn't buy each other Christmas presents. We talked about it and decided not to bother.'

Talking at the screening of the new puppet movie *Team America* in London, he said, 'She's a really nice girl and makes me laugh. She makes me very happy. We're both really busy so it can be hard to see each other sometimes. But we do the best we can and enjoy it when we do get to spend time together.'

The couple managed to spend some time together over Christmas, as Ashley was suspended for Arsenal's Boxing Day clash against Fulham, and, soon afterwards, Cheryl was spotted cheering him on during his return as Arsenal beat Newcastle, her home-town team, 1–0 at St James' Park.

'I had a bit of time off because I was suspended so I got to see Cheryl. But I spent New Year's Eve in a hotel with the rest of the team, preparing for the Charlton game. It's the same every year. You get used to it after a while.'

He also quashed rumours that the couple had got engaged and that he had bought her a ring, but added that he hadn't ruled out the possibility at a later stage. 'Despite what people say, we are not engaged,' Ashley said. 'We are both happy the way things are at the moment. But who knows what the future might hold? You never can tell. So we'll have to wait and see.'

If Ashley had left himself open to criticism for not buying Cheryl a Christmas present, that situation was soon rectified with Cheryl's announcement that at one stage over the festive period he had splashed out and bought her a £10,000 diamond necklace.

The heart-shaped pendant, from a Bond Street jeweller, contained no fewer than 80 diamonds. 'I'm really happy,' she said at one launch party. 'Ashley's the first serious boyfriend I've had in about two years. Things are going really well – he's so sweet. We don't go out to showbiz things much, so I'm feeling a bit nervous, but I'm just glad we're here together.'

However, a pattern was emerging. One minute Ashley seemed devoted to Cheryl; moments later there were other people, often attractive young women, on the scene.

Just 24 hours after Cheryl spoke of her happiness, Ashley

was spotted out and about at yet another trendy nightclub, the Attica in London, where he had been at a 22nd-birthday party for teammate Jermaine Pennant. Several newspapers reported that he turned his back and fled after he was spotted sneaking out of the club with two blondes. He had appeared to try to leave with the women when he saw waiting photographers and ran back into the club.

Moments later a man came out and told the girls to wait in the next street and Ashley then left by himself in a car with blacked-out windows.

A host of stars were also at Pennant's party, including Newcastle's Kieron Dyer, Spurs player Robbie Keane and George Best's son Calum. They toasted Pennant in his absence, as he had been advised to stay away after he was arrested for drink driving that weekend.

Far from being angry at nightclub sightings of Ashley with other attractive women, Cheryl was publicly totally relaxed about his behaviour

'I totally trust Ashley,' she said. 'It doesn't bother me when I see pictures of him coming out of clubs with girls trying to throw themselves on him, because I know he's not interested in them. I've had so many bad relationships. I'm not daft. I'd be able to sense it if there was something wrong. The moment I start believing the rumours and stop believing him, that's the time I'd have to end it. The most important thing is trust and honesty.'

She added, 'People will always have an opinion about our relationship. It's like when I heard about Charles and Camilla getting married. It's a weird one, because I really loved Diana. But I mean, if he's happy and he loves her then so be it. Ashley and I are not about to get married, but he makes me happy.'

As if to shout it to the world, Cheryl expanded on her love for the man in her life to writer Eva Simpson. 'I've never been this happy,' she said, playing, as she spoke, with the necklace that Ashley had bought her. 'The past year has been the best ever for me. I feel like I've got a fairy godmother watching over me. Ashley's my first proper boyfriend in two years, but I've never been in a relationship like this where I've been treated like a princess. Maybe it's because I was much younger before, but it's more likely that I kept picking idiot boyfriends. Valentine's Day was beautiful. Ashley ran me a lovely bath with loads of bubbles and candles and rose petals everywhere. He bought champagne and chocolates. It was really magical and he wrote the most gorgeous words in my card.'

Ashley had to miss a Valentine's Day clash with Crystal Palace through illness, and Cheryl explained, 'Ashley was really ill with this bad chest infection, which I think he caught off me, bless him. It was a bit of a downer for him, but it meant I had the most romantic day of my life.

'This is all so new to me. I keep thinking that there must be something wrong with him. I know I shouldn't think like that, but I just can't help it.'

At that time, 21 February 2005, Girls Aloud had a new album out, and Cheryl was reflective about the life she was now leading and the success she was having.

'Sometimes I yearn to wake up and be in my mum's

house and see my little dogs,' she says. 'But then I remind myself that I'm doing what thousands of young girls dream of doing. Life's so good. At the back of my mind I'm waiting for everything to come crashing down.'

Boys will, as they say, be boys, and so it follows that footballers will be footballers. They like nothing better than having some fun at a teammate's expense, so, when the rest of the Arsenal players heard that Ashley was dating one of the most attractive girls on the music scene, it was inevitable that he would become the focus of dressing room banter.

He would arrive for training and find magazines containing the latest photoshoot that Cheryl had done left on his seat in the changing room. The gigantic German goalkeeper Jens Lehmann couldn't resist cracking gags about when was Ashley, no great vocalist himself, going to join forces with Cheryl in a duet.

Another funster was the talented Dutch forward Dennis Bergkamp, who, Ashley wrote in his autobiography *My Defence*, would be next to Ashley in the treatment room reading magazines such as *FHM* and *Loaded* and would start going 'Mm, mm. Look at the woman in here.' That woman would, of course, be Cheryl and then he would glance in Ashley's direction and say, 'Sorry, Ash, didn't see you there.'

The obvious comparisons between a certain other footballer who played for England and a Premiership side and who had married a singer with an all-girl band were now being made, and more than once in magazines and newspapers the question was being asked: were Cheryl and Ashley the new Posh and Becks? Ashley wasn't quite in the Beckham glitz-and-glamour league – as a defender he hardly ever scored, which didn't help – and nor had Girls Aloud yet achieved the high profile of the Spice Girls. It didn't matter a bit. All the other ingredients were there: football, pop, youth, success – you name it, they had it in abundance.

Such was the interest now being generated that the media hung on every word. The slightest remark, if it shed the smallest light on their romance, would speed quickly around the world.

For instance, when Cheryl was promoting the band's single 'Wake Me Up' she let slip that she wasn't the noisiest girl in the world when the bedroom lights were off, saying, 'I think most men prefer to hear little breaths rather than big, loud screams, otherwise you sound like a porn film.' She added, for good measure, 'Sometimes you've just got to go for it and throw your man on the bed. Don't be embarrassed – do it with confidence.'

She couldn't resist referring to Ashley as 'gorgeous', adding, 'Things are going good for us. I'm so happy because I haven't had a boyfriend for two years. I'm just glad we're together and that my mum approves of him.'

Another magazine was told, 'Obviously, every girl wants a fantasy wedding. I would like a big, white wedding, but as for thrones and stuff – then no, that's not my style. I don't want to be a typical footballer's wife. I am fiercely independent. I like to have my own income, which most footballers' wives don't.'

That independence, the reluctance to automatically become one of the WAGs – the Wives And Girlfriends of soccer stars – was to be a recurring theme of many of the interviews she was to give in the coming months and years. It was something she obviously felt deeply about and was not reluctant to spell out to anyone who cared to listen.

By the start of May, Cheryl now felt confident enough in herself and in her relationship with Ashley – who was constantly being linked with a move to Chelsea – to announce, 'I think it's quite sweet that people call us the new Posh and Becks – I really don't have a problem with it at all. I admire David and Victoria – what they stand for is really good and they're nice people. It's nice people are interested in Ashley and me, but there will only ever be one Posh and Becks. I suppose you could think of us as a smaller-scale version of them, which is sweet. I'm definitely happy with that comparison.

'Everything is perfect with Ashley – it's quite scary how good it all is. I think the fact we are both in the public eye definitely helps – we understand what each other goes through. Ashley has had a hard time recently with all the transfer speculation and I really know how he feels. It's easier for us in that sense but it can be hard at times when people are trying to split us up, telling lies or whatever. But we're really strong – it's brilliant.'

She was so committed to the relationship, she said, that, even if there were rumours of other women in his life, she would always believe Ashley if he told her that he was innocent of any wrongdoing.

'We actually have a good laugh over some of the stuff people write. We sit and heartily laugh out loud together. But think when you start believing stories over your man, there are problems with the relationship anyway. I would always take Ashley's word over anyone unless I had solid, hard evidence something was definitely true. It just hasn't been an issue and it won't become one – we trust each other.'

The only thing, at that stage, that seemed likely to interfere with their relationship was, if anything, a light-hearted one: her support for her local team Newcastle United.

'I'm a Newcastle fan and when they play Arsenal I sit in the black-and-white side.

'I hope we beat them – but I secretly hope Ashley's OK with it. I totally take the piss if we beat them and he does the same to me even if we're playing against someone else. I give as good as I get.'

Her partnership with Ashley also meant, unfortunately, that she was now also exposed to the more unpleasant face of football: the hatred of rival fans. Ironically, she encountered it at Stamford Bridge and the fans involved were supporters of Chelsea, the club Ashley was soon to join.

But Cheryl's experience there was vastly different from what Ashley was to encounter when he eventually was transferred. She was reduced to tears by the supporters when she innocently asked for directions to the 'away' section of the ground.

'This big bald guy suddenly turned on me and started

shouting, "Arsenal? f***ing Arsenal? You f***ing Arsenal slag." His mates were all fat and bald and they joined in, calling me a f***ing slag. I was so scared. I was on my own and didn't know what to do. They were all shouting abuse at me. I just stood there in total shock. I was trying really hard not to cry in front of them.'

They eventually looked at her ticket and told her where to sit – but deliberately sent her in the wrong direction

'Stupidly, I took their directions and soon realised they'd sent me off in totally the wrong way. It took me ages to finally find my seat. It was awful. I'd never been to Stamford Bridge before and I don't think I'll be seeing Ashley play there again.'

Her ordeal had taken place before a 0–0 Premiership match and she had asked a stadium official for directions but had received no help.

She said, 'He recognised me and started shouting, "It's Cheryl Tweedy! Hey, everyone, look – it's Cheryl!" I was really embarrassed as I was on my own. Then I noticed everyone wearing Chelsea shirts and I couldn't see any Arsenal fans. So I walked on, found a group of Chelsea fans and asked if they could point me in the right direction to my seat. But I made the mistake of asking where Arsenal fans were meant to sit.'

It was obviously distressing for Cheryl, but there was a silver lining ahead as her relationship with Ashley was about to move to a much more serious level. Ashley had already been to Newcastle to meet her family. He'd been nervous about it, as any young man would be when meeting his girlfriend's parents, especially since Cheryl couldn't help but compare the situation to the hilarious hit film *Meet the Parents*, in which Robert De Niro plays a weird prospective father-in-law with massive reservations about the man his daughter is planning to marry.

He needn't have worried. Cheryl's father Garry was so taken with the young footballer that he was shortly to make a somewhat inebriated telephone call to him. Cheryl explained, 'It was so embarrassing. My dad phoned Ashley when he was drunk and was telling him, "I love you"!'

The Tweedys were described by one newspaper as 'a colourful bunch'. At that time Cheryl's sister Gillian had been bound over for affray and her brother Andrew had made several court appearances, also being bound over for affray, admitting stealing a motor scooter and tampering with a car while high on glue.

Ashley had been in the news too, but for all the wrong reasons. There had been massive newspaper coverage over his being 'tapped up' by Chelsea, who subsequently signed him, and he had been fined £100,000, later reduced, for his part in the affair.

He decided to head out to Chinawhite in London with pals, including Chelsea's Joe Cole, and Jermaine Defoe, Jermaine Jenas and Kieran Richardson. The players decided to cheer Ashley up by getting him out of his north London flat because Cheryl was away performing in Ireland. And, as he knocked back drinks, Ashley admitted that Cheryl had been a source of constant comfort to him during the inquiry into Chelsea's secret approach to sign him.

He told his pals, 'I'm so in love with her and I really miss her when she's not around. She's been there for me. It's been a really tough year.'

When he arrived at Chinawhite at around 11pm, he seemed in no mood to party. A source was quoted in one newspaper as saying, 'Ashley walked in with a face like thunder and was obviously still fuming about the verdict and the fine. The other players were having a laugh and joke, trying to cheer him up a bit, but he wasn't having much of it.'

They sat at a table drinking for an hour before Richardson, Joe Cole and Jenas headed for the dance floor.

The source said, 'Some of the players decided to leave Ashley alone as he was still pretty miserable. But Jermaine Defoe stayed with him, putting his arm around him and giving him a hug. Eventually, Cole started smiling and headed off for a dance.'

The footballers were among the last to leave the club at around 3.30am.

Meanwhile Cheryl and the rest of Girls Aloud had performed in Dublin on the last night of their tour. Earlier, she had been only too happy to talk about her man: 'We're madly in love. I think he's gorgeous. After the concert we'll go out for a couple of drinks with the girls and their boyfriends. We live in the same apartment complex in London, he just lives downstairs so that's how we met – I suppose it's handy. We've been together for eight months now but there are no wedding bells just yet. I'm too young to get married.'

Speaking while backstage before their Olympia Theatre gig in Dublin, Cheryl revealed, 'He treats me like a princess and buys me presents. But he doesn't spoil me too much – he keeps me on my toes. He's not your typical footballer lad at all, he's very quiet and shy. All the band get on really well with him.

'I've met his parents as well and they're lovely and I get on really well with them too, so that's good.'

Ashley, too, was talking as June arrived, making clear his plan was to 'get away and chill, get away from football', and adding that, as Cheryl had said she trusted him, so he trusted her: 'I'm not a jealous guy. I trust her 100 per cent. There will always be stories saying she is doing this or doing that.'

He was also vehemently denying stories that he was engaged to her. He was telling the truth about that, but it was soon all to change.

While Ashley was a little reluctant to go deeply into the question of his feelings for Cheryl, one of his Premiership pals was a little more forthcoming: 'Ashley thinks she's amazing. He says sometimes he looks at her and he can't believe that he's going out with her. He's so happy with their relationship he wants to take it further. They've been together for just under a year now and, even though they don't live together, they're a very solid couple, so he doesn't see the point in waiting around. After the tapping-up inquiry, it's made him realise just how important Cheryl is.'

According to the unnamed friend talking in a national

newspaper, 'Ash reckons the best way for him to bring happiness back to his life would be to wed Cheryl. She's been there for him and showed just how committed she is to him while they've been living under this cloud.'

If Ashley needed cheering up as the season ended and the brief close-season began, Cheryl also needed reassuring after bad news from Newcastle: there was a warrant out for the arrest of her 24-year-old brother Andrew. It was issued after he failed to turn up in court to be sentenced for mugging a teenager. He had admitted the charge but went missing the previous week after his girlfriend had had a miscarriage.

He and an 18-year-old friend jumped their victim from behind. The youth was knocked to the ground and savagely punched in the face during a 'long and sustained' assault. His attackers fled with a CD player and his mobile phone. He was treated in hospital for face injuries.

Tweedy, it was claimed, was the more violent. At Newcastle Crown Court, the other man's defence lawyer said, 'The court does not have the benefit of seeing Mr Tweedy but he is significantly more heavily built. It's always been the case he inflicted more harm.'

Andrew's friend had already admitted another late-night mugging an hour before the attack and had been sentenced to four years' imprisonment.

It was the sort of news that would put a damper on any holiday, but at least Cheryl had sun aplenty to take her mind off the situation back home – she and Ashley had gone to Dubai for their break. The tiny Gulf state had become a popular resort for footballers in recent years, the only drawback for them being that their chance to get away from it all fell in the months of June and July, when temperatures – hot all year round, anyway – practically soar off the thermometer scale.

Cheryl managed to find time to telephone one newspaper and repeat her familiar mantra: 'It really annoys me when people try to call me a footballer's wife. Footballer's wives have no career and live off their husbands' money. I was in Girls Aloud before I met Ashley and have my own successful career. I'm not going to quit the band and sit around in the sun all day or go shopping with Ashley's plastic. If I'm going shopping I'll pay with the money I have worked hard for.'

Cheryl – who had just been voted the sexiest footballer's wife or girlfriend by one lads' mag, had even turned down a suggestion to pose in a WAGs photoshoot for *Vogue* magazine.

She also insisted that reports that weekend that she was on the verge of quitting the band so she could spend all her time with Ashley were untrue. 'I'm not leaving the band. The story is absolute rubbish. Why am I going to walk away from Girls Aloud? We just finished our sell-out tour and our last album went double platinum. We're having an amazing time right now.'

On her return she was planning to go straight to the recording studio to record the girls' next album. 'To me it's not work at all. It's like hanging out with your friends for the day, every day.'

Cheryl and Ashley had now been together for nine months, had met each other's family, had been photographed *ad infinitum* and had their every move monitored. All that was as nothing compared with what was to follow once the news broke about what had taken place on the last day of that Dubai break.

Ashley and Cheryl were to get married.

3

THE PROPOSAL

What the world at large didn't know was that it wasn't just the blistering heat of Dubai in midsummer that had attracted Ashley. He had another motive: it was to be the romantic setting for his wedding proposal to Cheryl.

Four weeks before the end of the 2004–5 season, in which Arsenal won the FA Cup in a penalty shootout, with Ashley scoring one of the goals, he bought Cheryl a ring – and not just any old ring, either. The engagement ring had in it a single champagne diamond, often called the *haute couture* of the diamond world. One description of them states they 'are the most exotic, fashionable and alluring of natural-coloured diamonds. With soft, radiant tones, and exquisite shades from light champagne to deep, rich cognac and brown, champagne diamonds radiate natural warmth, sophistication and beauty that make them the perfect accompaniment to one's personal style.'

No wonder Ashley couldn't resist. Celebrities who have been adorned with champagne diamonds include Cameron Diaz, Jennifer Lopez and Kate Winslet. Now Cheryl from Newcastle was to join that group.

Ashley kept the ring, which reportedly set him back £50,000, hidden in his luggage waiting for the right moment to pop the question. When that moment came it almost turned into a farce. Almost, but not completely.

Ashley gave a frank description of the events leading up to the proposal in his autobiography.

The couple went on a safari approximately 60 minutes' drive from the city of Dubai and, at first, all seemed to be going well. In his mind Ashley had visions of champagne, romantic sunsets and gently sloping sand dunes. It was to be a cross between Rudolf Valentino in the silent film classic *The Sheik* and the sumptuous splendour of *Lawrence of Arabia*. The truth turned out to be a lot more prosaic.

No sooner had they arrived at their hotel villa and gone on the balcony to admire the view than a sandstorm began. Not many people in Britain have experienced a sandstorm – they are not too frequent in the United kingdom! – but they can cause havoc. Sunbeds were being whipped into the air, sand was stinging the eyes of anyone foolish enough to be outside and the overall effect was horrendous. The wind and the sand forced the couple to go inside to escape its harsh effects, but at least the noise of the storm gave Ashley cover for his next move.

He headed for the washroom in order to telephone Cheryl's father, Garry, back in Newcastle. Ashley had decided to play it the very traditional way and ask him for his daughter's hand in marriage first before putting it to the fiancée-to-be. He was so formal about the whole thing that he didn't even introduce himself as just 'Ashley'. Instead he said it was 'Ashley Cole' calling – something that Cheryl later ribbed him over. 'Cheryl's dad thought it was a big wind-up and that it wasn't me. I had to spend some time convincing him it was,' Ashley later admitted. 'In the end he realised it was for real and gave me his blessing. I was so relieved. It was very nerve-racking, but I knew it was the right thing to do.'

The main thing, however, was that he got the answer that he was seeking, a yes from his future father-in-law. By this time the storm had abated and so, in theory, Ashley was now able to pop the question. But the course of true love was not destined to run too smoothly. They clambered onto their respective camels and Ashley discovered that his hopes of being alone with Cheryl had been dashed: with them were a large group of other tourists and their children – hardly the perfect setting for a proposal of marriage.

To make matters worse, Cheryl was concerned about the welfare of the camels, which were tethered by their handlers. She felt that they must be suffering discomfort. Their nostrils would be tender because of the restrictions imposed on them and they would be suffering in the heat. Ashley, for his part, felt that camels would be capable of dealing with the temperature without too much trouble – they were camels, after all.

Writing about the proposal in his book *My Defence*, he said Cheryl continued to be worried about them until he said to her, 'Babe. Is there any way of you just shutting up?'

Cheryl, understandably, wasn't too thrilled to be addressed in this manner and, in spite of the heat, the mood was distinctly icy as the camel train – six beasts, ten adults and a sprinkling of children – set off.

The camels reached the halfway stage of their desert journey and everyone dismounted. They were to have champagne and strawberries as the sun set. Ashley and Cheryl, whose bad mood had abated by now, went a short distance away from the others.

He asked Cheryl to stand up and she agreed, although she was puzzled by the request. He then went down on one knee and said, 'I love you so much. Will you marry me?' She said yes and began to cry. Tears started to well in Ashley's eyes too and there, in the middle of the desert, they hugged each other. The others in the group began clapping the young couple when they realised what had happened. 'I had a big speech planned. But I just forgot all about it and said, "I love you so much, will you marry me?" ' Ashley would later recall of that moment.

Back at their holiday villa that night the couple began to make the wedding plans, with Cheryl at the forefront of the process. They quickly realised that, with their hectic schedules, this was not going to be an easy matter to arrange. There was a three-week window that they could utilise the next year after the 2006 World Cup had finished and at the end of the Girls Aloud UK 'Chemistry' tour. 'We couldn't wait to be Mr and Mrs Cole,' he wrote.

An event like that could not be kept secret. It was known that the couple had gone away together and pictures of Cheryl looking stunning in a skimpy white bikini were all over the newspapers. Their engagement was soon out in the open. Cheryl was ecstatic, saying, 'It feels fantastic. The ring is beautiful, it's a champagne diamond. He went down on one knee. He's a gentleman. It was all very romantic.'

A friend of the couple said, 'Cheryl said yes straightaway. Ashley has had it planned for a while now and he thought that the last night of their holiday would be the most appropriate time to do the deed. She got on the phone to everyone – her parents, family and of course her bandmates – Nicola Roberts was the first one as she is Cheryl's closest friend.'

A fellow passenger on their Emirates upper-class flight back to the UK from Dubai said, 'They couldn't keep their hands off one another on the plane until they fell asleep. As soon as it was time to get off they were hugging again.'

Cheryl's mother Joan was equally pleased: 'We are all delighted for her. Ashley is a lovely lad and we could not be happier for the two of them. They are such a lovely couple.'

Sadly, as often turned out to be the case throughout the two stars' relationship, there was a cloud about to block out the sunlight. The bad news came in the shape of a prison sentence being handed out to Cheryl's wayward elder brother, Andrew.

We have already seen how a warrant had been issued for

Tweedy's arrest after he failed to appear at Newcastle Crown Court. At virtually the same time as the news of the engagement was breaking, Tweedy was being sentenced to four years behind bars for a vicious street robbery.

It was said that Tweedy, then 25, and his accomplice Syd Rook pushed their teenage victim to the ground and used 'torture' techniques to make him hand over all of his belongings. Tweedy already had a string of previous convictions and had served a six-year sentence for stabbing two students.

The Crown Court was told that his latest victim, Kian Bradley, had been walking through Newcastle city centre on his way home from work when he was targeted in the early hours of 23 August the previous year, 2004. The 18-year-old victim was punched and beaten until all his possessions – just a portable CD player, mobile phone and £6 in cash – had been handed over.

Prosecutor Alec Burns said the two attackers were arrested with the victim's blood still covering Tweedy's hands. 'He was pushed from behind and tripped over the leg of one of the two people and then forced down onto his face,' he said.

The court heard how Bradley was then subjected to a series of questions, each of which was followed by a punch to the jaw. He was treated in hospital for the injuries to his face, which included bruises, swellings and deviated nasal bones.

Despite having the victim's blood on his hands, Tweedy initially claimed he had been tattooing a man called Dave when the robbery took place, but later admitted robbery.

He was due to be sentenced the previous month but, as we have seen, fled court before his case was called on.

Defence barrister Jane Foley said Tweedy was 'exceptionally remorseful' and told the court his offending was linked to drinking in excess as well as substance and drug misuse.

Judge Tim Hewitt jailed him for four years and said, 'You were in effect questioning him, some might say torturing him, and accompanying each question with a punch. It must have been quite an ordeal for him.' The judge said he had considered Tweedy's 'sad upbringing' and drug and alcohol problems.

Tweedy was sentenced to a further three months for failing to appear at the previous hearing.

As if that were not bad enough news, the next week Tweedy had his jail term extended for grabbing a police officer by the throat during a pub brawl. He appeared at North Tyneside Magistrates' Court to face four new charges, including criminal damage, a public-order offence and resisting arrest after trouble began at 11pm at the Cannon Inn, in North Shields. He had been put in handcuffs after shouting and swearing at other drinkers and police but he managed to wriggle free of the cuffs and grabbed an officer round the neck.

Alan Turner, prosecuting, said, 'There was a disturbance at the pub and Tweedy was shouting abuse and threats at a group of people. He was approached by a police officer and was shouting and swearing at the officer. He became violent towards the officer. He then became free from the handcuffs, injuring the officer's wrist, and had to be restrained by officers after grabbing one of them by the throat.'

Tweedy was given 14 days' jail for resisting arrest and a month's jail for a separate charge of failing to attend court. There was no further sentence for criminal damage or the public-order offence. He shouted obscenities at court reporters as he was taken away.

The news that her brother was jailed must have impacted on Cheryl, but she still managed to have a smile on her face at Chinawhite in Soho into the small hours with Ashley and some other members of the band as they celebrated her birthday with champagne and a chorus of 'Happy Birthday'. A source told 3am, 'Cheryl, Nicola and Kimberley were really letting their hair down. They drunk a lot of champagne and sung happy birthday at midnight.'

Ashley was so happy he couldn't refrain from admitting, 'I want to be with her for ever. People may say we got engaged too quickly or too young, but sometimes you know it's just right. When you find that right person you know they're The One and you just want to be with them for ever. That's how it is with Cheryl. I don't want anyone else.

'I'm leaving the wedding plans to Cheryl. She can have whatever she wants. I want it to be the happiest day of her life – a day she will never forget. We don't want it to be a big affair. All I care about is that our families, and, most importantly, Cheryl is there.'

The plan was that Ashley's brother Matthew would be

best man at the white wedding, but Ashley joked, 'I've left Cheryl in charge of the guest list – though I'm not so sure that's a good idea!'

Also at the birthday bash with Cheryl, Ashley, Kimberly and Nicola were dancers from the band's tour and songwriters, and the party-loving girls knocked back cocktails and Jack Daniel's with lemonade, as well as the bubbly.

Cheryl also showed off a £25,000 diamond bracelet Ashley had bought her and said, 'It's beautiful. He wanted to buy me lots of other things but I told him he didn't have to. I have everything I want in life – I'm getting married to him.' Whether she wanted it or not, Ashley also bought her a £45,000 brand-new BMW X5 for her 22nd birthday to replace her Toyota.

The so-much-in-love couple were already making plans for the wedding – and beyond: 'I definitely want big family. I've got three brothers and one sister so we'd like five kids,' Cheryl announced. 'I want a big, big wedding, with everyone there. I want a big dress, horse and carriage – a fairytale wedding. It's a once-in-a-lifetime event.'

The continuing stream of stories and public comment about the couple often mentioned the jewellery and gifts that they gave each other, not surprising in view of their success and the money they had available. But, in addition to emphasising their lifestyle, such information also acted as a beacon to those who wanted to take away such valuable items.

In the years that were to come there would be several

occasions when footballers homes were raided by thieves who were only too aware of the movements of the soccer players. If they were playing a match, they would not only be away from home but could even be out of the country, and that would allow ample time for the crooks to conceive and then execute their plans.

One such plot which became known to Cheryl left her terrified that her new, and much-publicised, jewellery was a possible target for three men who were planning to rob her.

She was given round-the-clock protection after advice from detectives, and security was stepped up at Princess Manor Park as a result. Police were called in by Arsenal after the club was alerted to the threat after announcing the couple's engagement.

A source close to the couple said, 'Cheryl is really shaken up. She has discovered that a gang have been plotting to steal her engagement ring and other expensive gifts given to her by Ashley. She has had reports that these men have been investigating every aspect of her life. They have been watching the nail salon she uses to build up a plan of her movements. Cheryl is terrified – and Ashley was worried sick when he found out. She has been told not to wear her engagement ring when she is out.

'Thankfully, Cheryl and Ashley are aware of what is going on and they now have adequate protection.'

Officers provided detailed security advice, including installation of a panic alarm. A Metropolitan Police spokesman confirmed sparingly, 'We are aware of a woman potentially being a target of a robbery.'

What made the threat so real was that, not too long before the scare, police had discovered a plan to raid Thierry Henry's home in Hampstead, although, once the scare had faded away, Cheryl proclaimed, 'I would have slapped them in the face with my shoes. They're scum picking on a young girl.'

The jailing of her brother and the threat to her safety were two matters of concern for Cheryl at what should have been one of the happiest times of her life. But there was an even greater tragedy to mar events that summer.

John Courtney was a gifted young footballer whose life had gone astray after he turned to drugs. He had also been a close friend of Cheryl's as she grew up in Newcastle. He died a short time before Cheryl and Ashley became engaged, curled up on a grubby carpet, still clutching the needle that killed him, a victim of heroin abuse.

His tragic death had a deep effect on Cheryl and she admitted it had turned her against drug use. 'It put me off for life. That nightmare devastated all John's family and friends. Seeing him in a coffin was terrible. And then to see pictures of [singer] Pete Doherty glamorising the habit, and with [model] Kate Moss on his arm, too. It makes me sick. Heroin is Devil's dust. It ruins lives and families and everything it touches.

'There were lots of users in my area. Heroin was there for the taking. I could easily have taken that route if I'd wanted to. But I always maintained my ambition and I'm proud of myself.'

John Courtney got hooked on heroin and turned to

crime to feed his £90-a-day habit. He was arrested and jailed for stealing.

Cheryl's career was taking off when she heard of Courtney's plight and she made an emotional visit to his house, pleading for him to quit. While there she wrote him a heartfelt letter reminding him of the lives he was destroying and begging him to save his own.

John's mum Angie said, 'He kept the note on his wall to remind him he had to keep battling.' Despite everything that she tried, three weeks after his release from jail, John injected himself with heroin for the last time. His body was found curled up on the floor of his uncle's flat.

Cheryl immediately sent floral tributes to John's parents and six sisters. Angie said, 'Cheryl's were among the first to arrive. This just shows how down to earth she is and how she'll never forget her roots. And to hear her speak out about drugs was fantastic. I just wish more celebrities would do it.'

Cheryl said, 'His mother crumbled to a five-and-a-half-stone wreck by the end, because he'd even steal Christmas presents from his family to feed his habit.'

The impact of her former schoolmate's death was so great that Cheryl was later to back an anti-drug drive by a local newspaper in Newcastle.

Cheryl was maintaining her links with Tyneside and returned to the city to launch a new lingerie range. As always, the talk turned to her forthcoming marriage. 'We are planning on getting married next year but we haven't set a date,' she told 3am. 'We haven't even set a month.

People keep asking about it, but I can't say any more than that.

'I've asked Ashley millions of times if he will come and play for Newcastle, but he never gives me a straight answer. I would love it if he did, though. I don't manage to get back home half as much as I would like to. I miss everything here. It's amazing how much my life has changed in the last three years. I can't do a lot of the things I used to want to do, but I'm doing what I love and that's what I wanted anyway.'

One thing that had been decided already by late summer 2005 was where the couple were to get married. The ceremony was to take place at Highclere Castle, the country seat of the Earls of Caernarfon, the Herbert family, and the largest mansion in Hampshire. The 6,000-acre estate had grounds built by Capability Brown

The house itself was built in the 'High Elizabethan' style similar to the House of Commons, using Bath stone, and had featured in a number of films and television programmes, ranging from *Jeeves and Wooster* to Stanley Kubrick's erotic thriller *Eyes Wide Shut*.

It had also been where Ashley's teammate Thierry Henry married his wife Nicole. Ashley and Cheryl had been to visit Highclere, and it seemed perfect, Cheryl falling in love with its elegance, space and design. That seemed to settle that until one day in September when Ashley was watching television at home and channel-hopping in the process. He saw something that immediately started to ring alarm bells in his head, news coverage of another wedding taking place at the mansion. It wasn't just any old wedding, obviously, and, given the status of the couple who were marrying, the coverage was massive. Jordan and Peter Andre were saying 'I do.'

It was the biggest celebrity wedding of recent years and left the 1999 wedding of David and Victoria Beckham, complete with their thrones, looking practically understated.

Jordan, a.k.a. Katie Price, wore a huge pink crown and a voluminous pink, crystal-studded gown while Andre sported hair extensions, a crystal waistcoat and stingray-skin shoes.

The bride arrived in a pink pumpkin-shaped coach and was greeted by a fanfare of trumpets and Jordan's three-year-old son Harvey, by footballer Dwight Yorke, walked down the aisle behind his mother.

The 300 guests included footballer Paul Gascoigne, Vanessa Feltz, Jenny Bond, actress Jennifer Ellison and Orlaith McAllister from *Big Brother*.

Among the bridesmaids were Kerry Katona, Liberty X's Michelle Heaton and Girls Aloud star Sarah Harding. Jordan made her entrance into the ceremony room to the accompaniment of a gospel choir singing Whitney Houston's 'I Have Nothing'.

The couple looked lovingly into each other's eyes and, shedding tears, exchanged vows in a civil ceremony before guests went on to a series of lavish receptions and dinner in a huge marquee. They both sported huge wedding rings – hers with 35 princess-cut diamonds, his with 20, and she said, 'It's so big I can't bend my finger.'

It was dubbed a 'super chav' event and 'with this bling I thee wed'. From all quarters it was criticised for its lack of taste and gaudy, over-the-top lack of style.

And it also put paid to any chance that Ashley and Cheryl would get married at Highclere. The sight of their proposed wedding venue being used by Jordan left Ashley open-mouthed. Ashley was later to write in his biography that Cheryl screamed at him, 'No way! Right, Ashley, we're changing venues.' He explained why: 'Every bride wants to be unique and original and Cheryl was no different. It would never have been "Ashley and Cheryl getting married at Highclere", it would have been "Ashley and Cheryl getting married at the same place as Jordan and Peter Andre".'

When news of their planned wedding location did leak out, sure enough the newspapers made the connection straightaway, mentioning that the happy couple would be following in Jordan and Peter's footsteps.

'In the world of celebrity,' he wrote, 'our big day would forever have been linked to that of another couple, so it left us with no option but to think again. It was a bit of a panic finding another venue at that late stage when there was no flexibility on our date, but the planners at Banana Split [a company famous for their up-market wedding arrangements] pulled out all the stops and we got what we thought was an even better, more romantic venue.

'We'd managed to get over that unexpected snag and Cheryl gave a massive sigh of relief. Our special day was back on track and we weren't going to be following in the wake of nobody. And the press would still think that Highclere was the venue, right up until the morning of the big day.'

It could hardly be said that the couple decided to 'downsize' once they had chosen their new venue They now plumped for Wrotham Park, just inside the M25, at Hertsmere in Hertfordshire. Like Highclere it had been used for a variety of films: *Gosford Park*, *Peter's Friends* and, again, *Jeeves and Wooster* had all shot scenes there

The couple wouldn't be doing too much of the planning themselves, however, as their wedding planners were the same company that had recently organised the bar mitzvah of the retail tycoon Philip Green's son in Cannes, persuading Beyoncé Knowles and opera legend Andrea Bocelli to perform for just 300 guests at the Grand-Hotel du Cap-Ferrat. It did cost £4 million for the package, mind you!

As the year drew to its close, Cheryl was busy with the rest of Girls Aloud promoting their album *Chemistry*. It sold more than 80,000 copies in its first week and was well reviewed, enabling Cheryl to say 'A lot of pop acts make a big splash with their first album and then fade away. We've done things the other way round. Our albums have got better and better. If we weren't here, people would be crying out for a group like us. Cheryl had an unusual use for the album cover of *Chemistry* too: she wrote a note of apology to Ashley on it.

The trouble had been that she often arrived home late after work and disturbed him, either when he was resting or when he was busy on his PlayStation. She wrote, 'Ash. Thanks for sticking by me, babes, and putting up with the early mornings when I'm banging around at half five and disturbing your sleep. Or the late nights when I come in and disturb your computer games! I can't wait to marry you.'

The marriage plans also dominated the conversation at the 30th-anniversary party for the charity Help a London Child at the Trocadero in the West End.

'I've got family who will never talk to me again if they're not bridesmaids. And my bandmates would probably not forgive me if they don't get to follow me up the aisle, too. I can't have ten bridesmaids, but I don't want to let anyone down. It's doing my head in, to be honest,' Cheryl admitted.

'I'm so excited about getting married,' she said, while keeping her cards close to her chest on the question of the venue. 'I want a huge meringue wedding dress. It's a tough choice between a fairytale one or a sleek one. I always thought I'd go for something more demure, but this is my big day so I'm going to go for it. I've already started looking – it's so exciting.

'It's not really sorted out, because this lot [the band] have had me working into the ground. I haven't had any time yet. Ashley's not helpful, either. You've got to be joking! He tries to play it like he's Mr Nice Guy, going, "It's totally up to you, babe, whatever you want." '

Nadine Coyle chipped in, 'We've been working so hard promoting the new album, *Chemistry*. So, when we get time off, we'll be burning the candle at both ends. We're making sure Cheryl's going out as much as she can before she gets married.'

Cheryl added, 'Who says I won't be going out when I'm married? What I love about Ashley is that neither of us wears the trousers – it's fifty–fifty. And with my past boyfriends it was me who called the shots. I'm gutted I won't be able to spend Christmas with him, though. He's working on Christmas Day so I'll go back and see my family in Newcastle. I might even go out on the Quayside [an area of Newcastle] with my mates.'

Ashley was one of those unlucky souls who have their birthday on or near Christmas. He was born on 20 December 1980, and so his celebrations were invariably in the midst of Yuletide frolics. That year was to be no different.

His bash was held at the Penthouse Club in the West End and Cheryl looked stunning when she arrived. She had every reason to: her dress was a £2,400 outfit designed by Victoria Beckham's favourite, Roberto Cavalli.

She relied on clever underwiring and cups to push up and hold her boobs together, but it didn't prevent a slight accident when she accidentally flashed a boob while getting into a car.

Ashley, as we have read, had been linked with a string of glamorous women in his young life, and that led Cheryl to lay down the law about who could, and who couldn't, come to the wedding.

'There is one of Ashley's ex-girlfriends that I'm pretty

sure won't be getting an invite. I don't want to name names, but I think she knows who she is. And there's no way I want her there on our wedding day.

'I'm not going to ban my ex-boyfriends from my wedding,' she laughed. 'I still talk to them and I'm sure Ashley speaks to his exes too. It really doesn't bother me because we trust each other completely.'

Those were among the final words she had to say in 2005 on the upcoming nuptials. It seemed hard, if not impossible, to accept the idea that 2006 would be an even more eventful year, given what had taken place in the 12 months preceding it. But it was going to be one in which the couple were hardly ever away from the gaze of the media. It was, indeed, going to be a year to be remembered.

4

HEADLINES AND
HARD TIMES

The news stories could hardly have been more eye-catching. Ashley Cole, a handsome young man who had been linked with a string of beauties over the years and who was engaged to one of the hottest (in every sense of the word) young women in show-business was suing two newspapers – over stories, he said, that labelled him gay.

It was a landmark court action that followed a *News of the World* article over claims that two anonymous top-flight footballers were involved in a 'gay sex orgy'. Ashley, who was not named in the article, decided to sue for harassment, breach of privacy and libel after rumours over his sexuality spread like wildfire on the Internet. He said the series of articles in the *News of the World* and the *Sun*, although not naming him, contained broad hints at his identity.

The *Guardian* newspaper reported, 'Legal experts view the case as an important step in taking the temperature of libel and privacy law in cases where the aggrieved parties are not named but the public is able to build up a "jigsaw" identification via tabloid hints that spark gossip via email, blogs and chatrooms.

'They said the privacy part of the claim was "unique" because it relied on an untested concept known as "false privacy" – even though Cole says he is not gay, he will argue his privacy has been invaded.'

'It's not a clear-cut case,' said Mark Stephens, media solicitor at Finers, Stephens, Innocent. 'It's difficult for both sides. But ultimately it's going to be embarrassing for the newspaper unless they were publishing on strong grounds.'

The original story, heavily trailed by TV advertisements the previous night, appeared in the *News of the World* on 12 February. Headlined GAY AS YOU GO, it claimed that 'two bisexual stars made some very dirty phone calls – using a mobile as a gay sex toy'. It also claimed that a reporter had seen a recording of the alleged incident. However, the newspaper did not claim to have a copy of the recording. It returned to the allegations the next week.

The tongue-in-cheek treatment continued in the News International stablemate the *Sun*, which later alluded to the story in the caption on a paparazzo's snap of the footballer out on the town with his pop star fiancée, Cheryl Tweedy, prompting a letter to newspaper editors by Cole's solicitors. At no stage did either newspaper name the footballer or explicitly use his picture, making the libel claim unusual. But legal sources believed he could have a strong case nonetheless.

'There is a risk when newspapers indulge in this sort of nudge-nudge, wink-wink insinuation that they will end up in court,' said David Engel, a partner at the law firm Addleshaw Goddard.

Several websites published the picture used by the *News of the World* to accompany its second story and suggested it was a crudely doctored version of a snap of Cole and a dance-music DJ taken from the website of a radio station, Choice FM.

The online gay publication *Pink News* featured a juxtaposition of the picture used in the tabloid and the alleged original, suggesting they were the same shot doctored by the paper.

Its editor, Benjamin Cohen, said he didn't believe Cole was gay but wanted to expose the methods of the tabloid and alert the media to the speed with which Internet rumours spread.

The *Guardian* added, 'Cole is likely to argue that the suggestion he is gay or bisexual is tantamount to accusing him of hypocrisy and thus damages his reputation.'

Ashley Cole's solicitor Graham Shear said it was 'disgraceful' that the England soccer star should face such 'insinuation and innuendo' before his wedding. Shear confirmed that legal proceedings had been launched against the *Sun* and the *News of the World* and added that Ashley was trying to focus on that summer's World Cup.

He said in a statement, 'These proceedings were commenced because these newspapers published false and offensive articles designed to tell readers that Ashley had behaved in what the *News of the World* described as a "perverted" way with other professional footballers. The newspapers knew there was no basis to name Ashley but arranged the articles and pictures in such a way that readers would identify him. There is no truth whatever in these allegations.

'Ashley Cole will not tolerate this kind of cowardly journalism or let it go unchallenged. It is disgraceful that he should be faced with this kind of unpleasant insinuation and innuendo at a time when he is trying to focus on this summer's World Cup and his forthcoming wedding. These proceedings will be vigorously and actively pursued.'

In the story published on 12 February, the *News of the World* had claimed two Premiership footballers used a mobile phone as a sex toy and subsequently the Internet had been awash with rumours about who was involved.

The newspaper published a follow-up story on 19 February, and similar allegations appeared in the *Sun*.

In case anyone thought that this was primarily a story of interest to those in Britain alone, the reaction to Ashley's actions would soon set them straight. News organisations from Canada to Australia, France to Singapore carried detailed accounts of what Ashley and his legal team were planning. The combination of show business, Girls Aloud and Premiership football – show business by another name – was irresistible.

Soon, Ashley's manager at Arsenal, Arsène Wenger, was expressing support for his player, who was sidelined through injury at the time.

'He wants to clear his name because he feels there have been some wrong rumours, and I can understand that,' said the Frenchman. 'Nobody likes to read these sorts of rumours in the newspapers about himself but unfortunately we are in a job where sometimes you have to face that, and you have to show mental strength'

'I feel that he is focused on his job, on doing well and recovering quickly. I do not believe that privately it is a problem, but maybe he has decided that because he is going to be married soon, he wants to go into something like that showing he cannot accept any insinuation on his private life.

'He did it completely privately. As a club we respect the private life of our players, and we do not interfere with that.'

Wenger praised Ashley for his mental resilience, despite suffering problems both on and off the field, including that fine for illegally talking to Chelsea about a transfer without Arsenal's permission.

'In my experience he has always shown mental strength when he is under pressure. He has never shown any weaknesses when he was in the public eye for negative reasons sometimes. When there have been things that might have distracted him, he has always shown remarkable focus on the game.'

Ashley was facing up to a fitness battle, having suffered another injury setback to a season that had been plagued with injuries.

He hurt his ankle early on in a reserve game against Tottenham, an appearance in which he hoped to build up match sharpness after many weeks out with a broken foot and then a thigh problem.

Both Wenger and England manager Sven-Göran Eriksson were hoping he would be back to full fitness well ahead of the final preparations for that summer's World Cup.

'I do not think at the moment that the World Cup is under threat. Certainly I would love to have him back now because he has only played seven games this season.'

Asked what kind of response a gay footballer would encounter, Wenger said a player's sexuality would make no difference to him. 'I don't mind the sexuality of a player. I mind the quality of his passing and how he behaves on the pitch. All the rest is of no interest at all.'

Ashley was later to say in his autobiography *My Defence*, 'Overnight, one wild rumour had become a newspaper innuendo, had become a Chinese whisper had become gossip in Internet chatrooms and websites. It was snowballing out of control and going nationwide as everyone seemed to gossip and snigger about the identity of "Player B".

'It was like I'd been thrown into someone else's nightmare by mistake.'

He said that on one occasion when he was putting money into a parking meter a stranger came up to him and said, 'You're gay, you are,' and walked away laughing.

'Not much bothers me. It takes a lot to get under my skin. But that got to me. I started worrying that the more people who read it, the more would believe it. I remember saying once to Cheryl that there can never be smoke without fire but this episode taught me that there can be smoke and not even one burning ember. Can you imagine if Cheryl weren't so understanding, weren't so trusting? Can you imagine the kind of hell this could have caused?'

In the midst of all these legal developments, there was at least one reason the couple could smile. Although Cheryl had said on numerous occasions that she did not wish to be considered as a WAG, she came top of a poll by *FHM* magazine, in which more than 100,000 readers voted, to select the sexiest footballer's 'wife'.

She was a long way ahead of rivals, including Coleen McLoughlin, Wayne Rooney's then girlfriend, and Alex Curran, gal pal of Liverpool midfielder Steven Gerrard, who was second.

Alex Curran was followed by *I'm A Celebrity* and former *Emmerdale* star Sheree Murphy, wife of Liverpool's Harry Kewell. Coleen managed only fourth place – and Victoria Beckham didn't figure in the list at all.

It was a welcome boost to Cheryl for, as the wedding day neared, the organisation of such a major event in her life was beginning to cause a strain: 'It's seriously stressful – it's like another full-time job. I've hired a wedding planner but all he ever does is call me and ask me to make more decisions. I feel like I'm living with a phone glued to my ear. Right now I'm starting to think I should jack it all in and Ashley and I should run off and elope somewhere. I just want it to be him and me, alone on a beach – but I know my mum would kill me if I did.'

Ashley's injury problems were continuing, in spite of her best attempts to get him fit.

'I've been doing my best to help him keep fit. We tackle each other in the bedroom, and he loves me massaging his feet.'

'He was really upset because he hasn't played for about six months now. It has been really tough for him. It would be like me losing my voice for six months – I can't imagine what it would be like. It was really bad for him. But he seems a lot more positive within himself now and I think he's going to be back within the next week or two. England really need him.'

In another interview, she added, 'There's still a lot to be done. Ashley is going out to the World Cup and I will be joining him. My mum keeps phoning me to make sure everything is on track.

'She's really excited and has taken a lot of stress off me. Thankfully we've got a couple of months when we get back from the World Cup, so I'll knuckle down and get it sorted.

'But to be honest if it wasn't for my family I would have run away and got married in Gretna Green.'

Cheryl admitted she hadn't picked her wedding dress yet but added, 'I know what I want but I can't decide on a colour.

'I'm not going to do a Jordan and have a big pink creation. I've gone for a smaller dress, and not in pink. It will be lovely, though. We're having the wedding in a castle, which is what I've always dreamed of since I was a little girl. We're having traditional wedding vows as well as ones we have written.'

Cheryl was about to start rehearsals for Girls Aloud's

UK tour, which opened in Nottingham on 22 May, but she had made sure the gigs would not clash with England's World Cup games and said, 'I'm definitely going out to Germany with Ashley. I told the other girls at the start that it's an important part of his life and I want to be there for him. I'd love it if he could be with us on tour, but obviously he can't.

'I've got a couple of weeks off after the tour so I can go and support him at the World Cup.'

She was still adamant, in spite of the *FHM* poll, that she had no intention of turning into a typical footballer's wife and she was appalled at the way many of them take their boyfriends' credit cards and rack up huge shopping bills. She added, 'I have my own credit cards. I would die of embarrassment if I had to resort to taking my boyfriend's cards. When I met Ashley, I was already earning my own money and doing my own thing. But I couldn't be like some footballers' wives and just go and spend all their money. You see girls in clubs making a beeline for the footballers and it makes me sick.

'I don't really go out much any more – I can't be bothered and I'm not a very good drinker. I went out one night while we were on tour in New Zealand and because I hadn't been drinking much it really went to my head. I was ill the whole of the next day, vomiting and feeling awful. I've said to myself that I'm not going to drink any more because I don't want to feel like that again. It's horrible. The other girls can drink me under the table. Sarah is really hardcore – she's a great drinker and she still always manages to look amazing. If I get drunk at a nightclub I can't bear the pictures of me in the paper the next day. Sarah is lucky – for some reason she always looks good.

'She'll go out with a bag full of makeup so that she's never caught out. I can't usually be bothered. I think it makes a difference that Sarah is single – she doesn't have a boyfriend to stay in with like me.

'I used to love going to parties and clubs but I think I've grown out of it now. I got bored of going to the same places, seeing the same people. It doesn't interest me any more.

'I don't like being drunk and losing control of what I'm saying or doing.'

Cheryl was talking in the run-up to the transmission of a warts-and-all documentary on television about the girls, and she added that she was shocked when she watched a tape: 'I'm a little bit appalled at my language, to be honest. I'm shocked at how much I swear. I don't like it. Maybe we should get a swear box on the Girls Aloud tour bus. We'd probably be millionaires by the end of the tour!'

World Cup fever was mounting by this time, with interest in England's pursuit of the trophy ranging from the fascinated to the downright hysterical. There were almost as many articles on the WAGs as there were on the team itself. And no matter how much Cheryl tried to distance herself from that label, it was being well and truly applied to her; there was no escaping it.

There were even lengthy items on the hotel in Germany where the 'England team' would be staying – the WAGs, mind you, not the players. The WAGs were to be in a completely different resort, the Brenner's Park Hotel in Baden-Baden, Germany. Dating back to 1872, it has been described by an observer as 'stately and genteel, luxurious and expensive, but it would be more at home in Harrogate than Hollywood. Its usual clientele is more footballers' grannies than *Footballers' Wives*.

'Bedecked with crystal-glass chandeliers, French antiques, chintzy wallpaper and white Carrara marble bathrooms, it looks, on the surface, as if it could have been designed by those behind the popular ITV television series *Footballers' Wives*.

'It has not one, but two beauty spas, offering a bewildering array of treatments including more than 30 different massages, 10 different facials, numerous pedicures, manicures, peels, scrubs and fitness regimes.

'Anyone feeling particularly adventurous can hire a 'spa butler' who will gladly organise a four-handed Thai massage or a session of 'body torture' – an hour of bending, twisting and pummelling which, apparently, is good for you. A special menu boasting only 700 calories a day can be cooked up by the hotel's nutritionists for those worried about their weight.'

But the atmosphere at the hotel, down the road from the fortress-style Schlosshotel Buhlerhohe, where the England players were holed up, was more akin to a tea dance than a Manchester nightclub.

Most of the guests, who were well past retirement age, would sit quietly through meals in the Wintergarten restaurant, only occasionally offering polite applause to Frederico, the in-house pianist tinkling his way through prewar classics. The mahogany Oleander bar may have offered Moet et Chandon brut rosé at £320 a bottle but you wouldn't see it being drunk out of high-heeled shoes.

Baden-Baden had Germany's highest proportion of millionaires per capita, and one wit couldn't resist pointing out it probably had the highest number of Zimmer frames, too. In spite of its affluence – the casino still had a solid-gold roulette wheel left over from its Napoleon III heyday.

With all the talk of court cases, weddings and WAGs, it might have seemed to some that football was taking a back seat in Ashley's life. Nothing could, of course, be further from the truth.

Injury had devastated his season and cast a shadow over his immediate future. Nevertheless, Arsenal had made it to the final of the Champions League and faced the mighty Barcelona in Paris. Ashley was fit again and with Mathieu Flamini unfit he was in the team again.

That gave him the opportunity to reflect openly on the eventful 12 months he and Cheryl had been through since that proposal in Dubai.

'To walk out in the Champions League final will make me a very happy man. Because I have been out for so long, I owe the lads one. It's been a tough season for me. I have never been out for so long. It played on my mind. I did think my season was over. I wasn't playing for Arsenal and that meant I wouldn't be involved with England.

'I had already been out for three months with a foot problem and then I did my thigh and then my ankle. I thought I was finished. It's every player's nightmare. You want to play – and to have that taken away is horrible. But I have an awesome family behind me and a very supportive girlfriend, who has stuck by me when I was starting to be annoying. If anyone thinks I moan on the pitch, they haven't seen what I'm like when I'm injured and not playing. I'm bad. It's hard for me to watch the team when I'm like that.

'When I'm at home, my girlfriend and my mates keep me going, but it gets worse when I come into the club. Sitting in the physio room while everyone else is playing hurts. But the lads made sure I kept my spirits up. I feel sorry for Flamini and I know how he feels. It's a dog-eat-dog world, though.'

On the eve of the big European match Ashley had played only 14 games in the season and his last England appearance had been in the humbling 1–0 defeat by Northern Ireland in Belfast.

He was anxious to make up for lost time with Arsenal and with England under their Swedish coach Sven-Göran Eriksson.

'Sven was speaking to me all the time. He has been calling the physios and seen the reserve games. I don't think a lot of national bosses would do that. That was pleasing because a lot of people had written me off. I spoke to David Beckham as well and it's nice to know the others want you there in Germany. I never received any assurances from the manager here that I was his first choice No. 3, but it isn't all about me. He has other things to think about. I wasn't surprised or shocked about that.

'To be honest, I was so grumpy, he was probably sick of my face. I missed playing and wasn't going to be happy unless I was playing. This season has been very tough mentally and to come back at this stage is amazing. To win the World Cup would be, too. I feel fine at the moment. Although I am not as sharp as I want to be, I'm getting there and, with the England matches coming up I should be raring to go. Of course it's a worry that the injuries may come back. Every day before training I check the ankle to make sure it's OK. The Arsenal medical team have been great.

'To win the Champions League would be incredible for the club. It could be the start of a new era at Arsenal. To go into the new stadium as European champions would be a great boost. I played against Ronaldinho at the last World Cup. He did one of his step-overs and nearly put me on the floor. He is an amazing player, but I would always go for Thierry Henry – he doesn't get the credit for how many goals he sets up. And the ones he scores are always special. He is one of the best ever – a great skipper and a great person. You know that as captain he will give us something extra and we always think he will win us the game. If he does eventually leave, I would love to do the job of captain one day.'

5

WORLD CUP WAGS

There was a time, many years ago, when the World Cup finals were simply about football and deciding which nation, for the ensuing four years, could announce that it had the best national side in the world.

Those days were long gone by the time the 2006 finals in Germany were getting under way. Yes, the football was still there, of course it was, but so were elements of commercialisation, product-placement, branding and television viewing figures that were measured in billions. And it was 'showbiz' too, of that there was no doubt.

It was remarkable that Ashley, after such an injury-hit season, was there at all for the four-yearly feast. He had played in the Champions League final against Barcelona, where a brave Arsenal display – they were down to ten men for most of the game – saw them eventually lose to a marvellous Barcelona side.

He talked openly again of his achievement in making it to Germany just days before the kick-off and England's opening gamer against Paraguay.

He had been through a succession of injuries that year after suffering a stress fracture of his foot back on 2 October in a 1–0 victory over Birmingham City. He returned in the 7–0 thrashing of Middlesbrough on 14 January but injured his thigh and was out again.

He thought those problems might have been behind him by February but then he damaged his ankle in a reserve game against Spurs. 'It was the worst time of my career. The Tottenham reserve game was the lowest point.

'I was fully fit coming back to that. Then in the first five minutes I badly sprained my ankle. That was as bad as it got. I was on crutches and thinking to myself, "I am not going to make it to the World Cup." I was on crutches for two weeks and I had a scan.

'The doctors thought I had chipped a bone. I was devastated at that time. But it turned out to be not as bad as they feared and now I don't even think about it. I have a good family, good girlfriend and good teammates.

'I couldn't allow myself to become too depressed because I wanted to be at the World Cup so I had something to go for, something to hang onto.

'Every footballer who is not playing is going to be down. I was watching players go out and training and was sitting in the gym doing weights.

'But I had strong people behind me to help get me through it. There were times when I didn't think I would make it. I was out for seven months and it's been hard. I was down. Every player is when they are not playing.'

It wasn't until 1 May that he managed to make his comeback, when he returned to the field as a substitute against Sunderland. Astonishingly he only played three games for Arsenal, including that defeat by Barcelona, before the World Cup finals. Ashley safely came through England's 3–1 midweek friendly triumph over Hungary and the 2–1 B international defeat to Belarus five days later but was fully aware that he was still a little rusty.

'I am not there yet but I am getting closer. I was out of action for seven months and it has been hard for me. I am a little happier now. I can't wait to get on the plane to Germany. I would prefer more games. My fitness is all right and I feel good. I'm not 100 per cent with my touch, but the more games I play, the more it will come back.

'Against Hungary I took a few belts, but I came through it without a hitch and so I'm happier than I have been for a long time. Being out for seven months wasn't a happy time for me, naturally.

'I'm just trying to train hard. You can't keep thinking about the negatives all the time, even though it was the worst time in my career.'

England's chances of winning the trophy were constantly being analysed, but there were times that the football seemed to be taking second place in the media to the obsession with the WAGs. There were continued analysis of who was the most attractive, best dressed, fanciable and so on.

One poll placed Cheryl fourth, behind the England

manager's squeeze, Nancy Dell'Olio, and above Mamen Sanz, the beautiful wife of the Spanish striker Raoul, adding, 'Wonder what Ashley Cole will listen to on his iPod as he whiles away the hours in Germany? Cole will take some ribbing from his teammates, but has little option other than to tune in to Girls Aloud, the made-on-TV band featuring his fiancée, Cheryl Tweedy. The feisty singer, who met Cole in a nightclub (now there's a big surprise), wears a £50,000 engagement ring given to her by Cole last year.

'According to Tweedy, the gallant Ashley proposed on one knee in Dubai after they had been on a camel ride. Bless him. No prizes for guessing who is the boss – Tweedy was sentenced to community service after a conviction for punching a lavatory attendant in … a nightclub.'

Unkind to mention that nightclub incident after all those years, but it was something that Cheryl would have been used to by now, that fleeting moment coming back to, if not haunt her, then certainly remain as a blot on her copybook.

None of that seemed to matter, however, as the WAGs headed for Germany by that most un-WAGish of routes, a Ryanair flight from Stansted to the tiny Karlsruhe-Baden-Baden airport.

It was a Friday afternoon, the day before England started their campaign with a game against Paraguay, and the girls' every move was being monitored in almost forensic detail by a nation agog with every move they made, albeit with a slight tongue-in-cheek fascination at times.

At the airport, normally home to thousands heading out on week-long package tours or taking advantage of cut-price flights, Cheryl said, 'I didn't realise we were flying with Ryanair. I think it's quite funny. I've got to pop back for a few gigs and things but I'll be there for all the games,' she said. 'I think they'll win it. I'm very confident. Ashley's forgotten the charger for his mobile. I've got it in my bag. He's very confident. He had a massage last night after straining his thigh but he's fine. I'm looking forward to giving him a celebratory hug after the game tomorrow. I just hope he's booked us into a nice hotel.'

She was joined by Joe Cole's girlfriend Carly Zucker, Paul Robinson's wife Rebecca and daughter Lucy-May, Jermaine Jenas's mother Lynnette, Wayne Bridge's French girlfriend Vanessa Perroncel – who was to generate an avalanche of headlines of her own some years later over her friendship with several of the Chelsea team – Michael Carrick's girlfriend Lisa Roughhead, and David Beckham's mother Sandra.

Cheryl wasn't the only one with butterflies in her stomach: Vanessa Perroncel said, 'I am so excited. I am feeling very excited and can't wait to see the match. I have spoken to Wayne this morning and he seems to be very relaxed and said everybody wants to get started. I think we get to see them after the game and I can't wait. I hope England play France in the final – then I can't lose.'

Peter Crouch's girlfriend, aspiring model Abigail Clancy, boarded the plane after buying a bikini in the airport. Not too surprisingly, many of the party had to reach for their credit cards to pay for excess baggage before they could board the flight.

The WAGs' arrival at their luxury hotel merited blanket coverage. The staff stood to attention as Coleen McLoughlin, Wayne Rooney's girlfriend, arrived after turning up in a 60-foot luxury coach with Alex Curran, 23-year-old fiancée of Steven Gerrard. They had travelled together from Frankfurt airport with friends and family, including Coleen's mother Colette.

Dressed in blue jeans, brown top and large, dark sunglasses, 20-year-old Coleen laughed and joked as she wheeled two huge suitcases and two large holdalls on a trolley. Alex, dressed in blue jeans, a white top and sunglasses, brought her two year old daughter Lilly-Ella. Coleen and Alex had reportedly already started their spending spree by flying in two 'tan therapists' at a cost of £15,000.

One noticeable absence from the party, temporarily at least, was Victoria Beckham, whose plans were hit by a three-hour delay at Madrid airport after engine failure on her flight.

The local Gucci and Hermès boutiques in Baden-Baden had ordered an extra £200,000 of clothes and accessories to tempt the new arrivals.

A source said, 'With so many glamorous women in the same place, the shops wanted to make sure they didn't run out of stock. They are anticipating a lucrative few weeks and hope that England do well.'

Red and white England flags had been hauled up around the town to welcome the WAGs. At bus stops there are billboards carrying the greeting, 'Welcome to Baden-Baden, Victoria.'

At their hotel the England flag was flying at the front of the hotel. In the garden, red and white flowers, specially planted, were in full bloom.

Among the other WAGs in town by this time were Emma Hadfield, who was engaged to Manchester United's Gary Neville, and Melanie Slade, girlfriend of Arsenal teenager Theo Walcott.

Slade spent one afternoon with her father Don in the town's coffee shops.

One newspaper summed it up with this description:

The women are here for the most important competition in the world – to decide which of them is 'Queen of the Wives'.

Victoria Beckham holds the title but she is keenly aware that Miss McLoughlin is after her crown. So too is Nancy Dell'Olio, who wants Sven-Göran Eriksson's last World Cup as England coach to be a spectacular triumph (for her).

Other high-profile WAGs include the girlfriend of Ashley Cole, Cheryl Tweedy, 22-year-old singer with the band Girls Aloud. Her look is what you might call overt.

Even on the day of the match, the *Sunday Mirror* reported:

They're ruthlessly competitive, spent months preparing for this moment … and honed their bodies to perfection.

No, not the England team – their wives and girlfriends. But competition between England's affectionately named WAGs is fiercer than a Brazil–Germany final.

Yesterday, as they set off from the five-star Brenner's Park Hotel in Baden-Baden for the first England game of the World Cup, captain's wife Victoria Beckham led the fashion parade out of the hotel and onto the coach for the two-hour drive to Frankfurt.

Queen Bee Victoria managed to retain her crown in skin-tight white jeans emblazoned with the St George's Cross, teamed with a skimpy white vest. Ashley Cole's fiancée, singer Cheryl Tweedy, followed suit with white jeans and a vest.

Her man Wayne Rooney didn't play yesterday, but fiancée Coleen McLoughlin didn't sit it out in the fashion stakes.

Steven Gerrard's fiancée Alex Curran, who gave birth only last month, also squeezed into skin-tight jeans. Determined to have the biggest hair, Alex was snapped on her hotel balcony with huge curlers.

The newcomers to the WAGs team – Peter Crouch's other half Abigail Clancy and Theo Walcott's teen sweetheart Mel Slade – also looked fabulous as they boarded the coach.

The fact that England won that rather dull opening match 1–0 seemed almost secondary to the updates that kept emerging from Germany on how the WAGs were coping.

The game did at least give Cheryl a chance to have a long conversation with Victoria Beckham. The England captain's wife had 'been there, done that and bought the T-shirt' when it came to handling the fame that went with pop stardom and simultaneously being the love of a soccer star's life.

'Cheryl was so impressed with the organisation of the recent Beckham pre-World Cup ball, Full Length and Fabulous,' one of the England girls' friends announced, 'that she has asked Victoria if she could give her tips for her own wedding and reception. Victoria believes that accessories are everything and that they will be the icing on the cake so to speak. Victoria and Cheryl will be spending a lot of time together at the World Cup to help thrash out the arrangements for Cheryl's big day. There will be a lot of having spas together and going for walks in the grounds of the hotel.'

Wayne Rooney's fiancée Coleen led England's ladies on a night out to celebrate victory over Paraguay. Coleen, Alex Curran and Melanie Slade, danced on the tables of a packed bar until 4am. And they were joined in the frolics by Abigail Clancy and Elen.

Around ten England girls plus pals flocked to the Garibaldi Bar in Baden-Baden.

Coleen's 44-year-old mum Colette joined in the fun, bopping the night away on a table. Carly Zucker also leapt on the table and was joined by 28-year-old Elen, who raised a glass to the party.

They belted out a string of songs by crooner Barry White

and ran up a bar bill of about £400, knocking back champagne and vodka and Red Bull.

An onlooker said: 'They clearly thought singing hits by the Walrus of Love would get them in the mood for love the following night. The girls looked as though they were having the time of their lives. They were clearly in a mood to celebrate England's win and were really rocking. All heads turned when they came in because they were such a stunning bunch of girls. It was terrific to see them out enjoying themselves.'

The girls – but not Victoria Beckham, who stayed with sons Brooklyn, Romeo and Cruz – finally tottered out singing 'Football's Coming Home' amid gales of laughter.

They hardly seem to notice when one cheeky fan in a Rooney No. 9 shirt dropped his shorts beside them.

The exhausted girls then enjoyed a lie-in at the Brenner's Park Hotel before spending the Sunday with their men.

Eriksson had allowed players and their loved ones a free day to come and go as they pleased and dine either at the team's Schlosshotel Buhlerhohe in the Black Forest or elsewhere.

Many stars spent the day relaxing with their wives and families in town and a smiling Ashley was spotted strolling around town with Cheryl.

The manager too had some female company. Nancy Dell'Olio said, 'I will keep him happy as much as I can, but I think the players and the results can keep him very happy. It is essential to be loved and to make love. Everyone might think that is sex, but I think it can be much more romantic than that. It is much better if it is evolved.

'Everyone agrees there is nothing better in life – it's the only thing that makes the world go round right.'

A Football Association (FA) source said, 'The mood in the camp is sky-high. And morale will climb even higher with the arrival of the wives and girlfriends for the night. We're in great shape physically and mentally.'

Victoria and Cheryl's bonding continued as the pair dined together in the Medici Restaurant at the hotel while the other WAGs were at a different table.

Nancy Dell'Olio was also dining at the same restaurant – at a third separate table

And they had all booked their tables well in advance, with the restaurant's acclaimed sushi chef coming in on his day off. The meal he prepared was a low-key affair, lasting just under an hour and cost just €69.80 for sea bass, sushi, two diet cokes and an €8 bottle of Evian water. They left a €5 tip on top of their bill.

Cheryl and Victoria popped their heads around a corner of the restaurant to say hello as they were leaving.

Coleen McLoughlin spent hundreds of pounds in ten minutes in one boutique, buying Gucci and Christian Dior shoes before forking out for a Dolce & Gabbana shirt and blouse. The girls also spent £1,700 on designer clothes in Monika Scholz before heading next door to Albert, where they bought several pairs of £500 designer sunglasses each.

Elen Rives said, 'We are here to support the boys. But it's nice to do some shopping.'

Such was the interest shown in Cheryl and the other girls that at times the football seemed almost secondary. England had several days between their matches when, soccerwise, very little was happening. The shops, however, were open every day, and so were the restaurants and bars. Journalists with little to write home about on the pitch had a ready-made reserve lined up in the WAGs – and they were prettier, too

It had reached such absurd levels that the on-field rivalry between Germany and England was transferred to a battle between the ladies in the lives of the players.

The first strike was from Germany's top-selling newspaper *Bild*, which mocked David Beckham's wife, mother, sister and children.

The article said Beckham's wife Victoria was a 'luxury wife'. It called two of Becks's three sons dwarves, and dubbed another son, Romeo, a girl.

It also described his mother as having 'a farmer's smile' and his sister Joanne as 'Chubbyham'.

'Oops, is she plump,' the paper wrote. 'Arms, breasts, bum – very British. Joanne is one of those who drinks sangrias on a Mallorca beach out of buckets. And after that the first to dance on the table – topless.'

British tabloid the *Sun* responded quickly, splashing the headline HOW DARE THE GERMANS ATTACK BECKS BIRDS? across its front page, with a picture of Victoria Beckham, labelled 'The Beaut' next to a portly, lederhosen-clad German barmaid called 'Das Boot'.

On its website, the paper also asked, 'While the England

players' wives and girlfriends include stunners like Posh Spice, Coleen McLoughlin and Cheryl Tweedy, can anyone name a partner of the German footie stars?' The *Sun* even organised a readers' poll to discover who the men and women of Britain thought was the 'fittest WAG'. Cheryl won it by a large margin: 31 per cent of the votes, more than double Abigail Clancy in second place and ahead of Carly Tucker's 13 per cent. Victoria Beckham merited only 8 per cent while Coleen McLoughlin was a mere 4 per cent. Perhaps that came as a welcome boost for Cheryl, who apparently wasn't too happy with her figure, telling one questioner, 'From the waist down it all goes a bit wrong. I would like to firm up my legs.'

Many observers were commenting on the way Victoria seemed to be advising Cheryl on how to cope with football and pop music, but others placed a different interpretation on it. Ever since Ashley's talks with Chelsea there had been speculation about his leaving Arsenal. David Beckham was playing for Real Madrid at the time so, two and two must make … 'Cole for Madrid.' It was, of course, a transfer that didn't happen, but that summer, amid the heat of the Black Forest, it all seemed very plausible indeed.

'You'll love it in Madrid – and you'll have us, too,' Posh allegedly told her. 'When we went, we didn't have anyone to start with. I'll show you the best places to go, and put you in touch with the best estate agents. It'll be great.'

It seemed a mutual admiration society. Cheryl, when asked by one passer-by who of all the WAGs she though had the most style, had no hesitation in replying, 'Victoria is the most stylish. She always looks amazing to me. I love her Rock and Republic jeans, too. She gave me a pair when she first started designing them and I've bought loads more since then. They're expensive but, believe me, they're worth it.'

Cheryl, dressed in skimpy denim hot pants that showed off the barbed-wire tattoo on her thigh, also cheekily revealed what she thought about those 'sex and football don't mix' theories when she said, 'I've heard sex before a big game can leave footballers drained. But I'm definitely not following those rules.'

She wasn't among 'the usual suspects' when the WAGs went out on another 4am nightclub bender, preferring not to accompany the group, but Cheryl was one of a six-strong party when a total of £55,000 was reportedly spent in an hour.

A total of £3,000 worth of shoes and shirts were bought at the trendy Monika Scholz boutique and other items on the shopping list were £6,000 Chloe bags, £1,000 Diane von Furstenberg dresses and £1,000 Prada shoes, although the discreet German boutique owners kept the identities of their new best customers a secret and would not say who bought what.

One boutique owner said, 'It is almost as if they want to shop the place dry of designer clothes. More money is being made in our fashion shops than anywhere else during the World Cup in Germany. I hope that England remain in the tournament for a long time!'

Ilona Dressel-Witte, owner of Nanou – one of Baden-

The dream couple – Cheryl and Ashley set out to celebrate her 25th birthday.

Top: Cheryl has a talent to entertain even at 13.   *Mirrorpix*

Bottom left: A kiss from mum Joan with her dog.   *Alamy*

Bottom right: Girls allowed a snack. Cheryl, Sarah and, nearly Aloud, Javine.

Rex

Girls Aloud – Kimberley, Nadine at the back and Cheryl, Sarah and
Nicola at the front.

Alamy

Above: Ashley warms up for a game. *Mirrorpix*

Below: Celebrating at the Champions League match on 10 March 2009 against Juventus. *Cleva*

Top left: Raising the silver for Arsenal.   *Mirrorpix*

Top right: All smiles with Chelsea.   *Cleva*

Bottom: Contemplating the future.   *Mirrorpix*

Top: Ashley and Cheryl started their relationship in 2004. *Rex*

Bottom left: Pop singer and footballing star. *Big Pictures*

Bottom right: Cheryl and Ashley were to be engaged on holiday in Dubai.

Big Pictures

Left: Cheryl has friends in high places – even Prime Minister Gordon Brown came out for Comic Relief.

Below: Victoria and Cheryl out together.

Rex

Top: At the World Cup Quarter Final in Germany 2006, England played Portugal. Beckham's son Brooklyn, Cheryl and Victoria watch on.

Bottom left: Ashley and Cheryl had their wedding reception at Wrotham Hall in July 2006.

Bottom right: Cheryl and Nicola with famous friends Elton John and David Furnish.

Rex

Baden's designer boutiques – said, 'They're doing a lot of shopping. They come every day, apart from Posh, who we've not seen. They all want clothes. They love Blumarine, Chloe, Marni. They all have very good taste.'

Dressel-Witte added that the WAGs were the perfect customers: 'They're so polite and they spend a lot of money.' Peter Malassr, co-owner of the nearby Monika Scholz boutique, said, 'The ladies love the labels we have here.'

England had progressed through to the last 16 of the tournament, so it was time for the WAGs to celebrate – again – before the match against Ecuador. They went out on a £5,000, champagne-fuelled, seven-hour celebration ahead of the game. And, as they hit a bar in town, the girls sang out rousing choruses of 'We're not going home!' The girls got through bottle after bottle of bubbly and scores of spirits and cocktails at the Garibaldi bar.

And they stunned onlookers by dancing on chairs as fans sang terrace chants for their fellas. Those letting their hair down included Coleen, Alex, Lisa Roughead, Nicola, Carly, and Elen Rives. Victoria had left Germany for 'business reasons' and Nancy Dell'Olio and Cheryl ducked out for an early night at 1am.

As fans in the bar sang chants to each of their boyfriends in turn, the girls stood up to take the applause.

There was another party, too, this time for Ashley's mother Sue, who was 50 the day before Cheryl's 30 June birthday. Sue thought she would be having a quiet dinner for two with Cheryl, but a surprise party had been organised for her. Ashley even managed to get some brief time off from the England camp and arrived carrying a birthday cake.

There was a chorus of 'Happy Birthday' when Sue walked into the bar after dinner with Cheryl. The girls then sang Spandau Ballet's 'Gold' changing 'Gold' to 'Cole' in honour of Sue's boy Ashley. Delighted, Sue stood up to lead the singing and one onlooker said, 'It was a real blow-out, but they wanted to have a big night out for Sue and all get together before the game.'

That particular bash may not have captured too many headlines, but by now the girl followers had been dubbed 'Reservoir WAGs' over their antics.

Sources at the group's hotel in Baden-Baden have claimed the atmosphere is 'not unlike a blinged-up *Big Brother*'.

The insider explained, 'The WAGs are all exhibitionists who know they're on camera. At first it was all nicey-nice but then their characters start to show. The competitiveness and bitching is growing ever more intense.'

Victoria Beckham, Nancy Dell'Olio and indeed Cheryl weren't too much to the forefront; on some nights they weren't there at all. But the girls continued enjoying themselves.

Coleen McLoughlin reckoned it was good for the players too because having family around stopped them getting bored. 'I know some past England managers have not approved of the players' wives and girlfriends being at the World Cup camp. But we have all been saying how good it is that times and attitudes have changed and we can go along to watch the lads. And I enjoy spending time with

Wayne. He loves watching the other games on the telly, but it's good for him to switch off for an hour or so and rest. It's definitely good for morale, especially because some have children and their dads would be climbing the walls if they were stuck in the hotel without seeing them.

'I know John Terry likes to see as much of his new twins as he can.'

All of this may seem trivial, but in the background there was a much more serious matter to be settled. Ashley had announced his legal action against the *News of the World* and the *Sun* earlier in the year. In March lawyers acting for him had taken the unusual step of 'recruiting' people who read those newspapers to act as witnesses for him in his libel action against the two papers.

His legal team launched a special online survey at Ashleycolesurvey.com that asked readers if they read any of the series of stories in the two papers in the between 12 and 19 February, claiming that a 'well-known DJ' had taken part in 'perverted' and 'debauched romps' with two unnamed Premiership footballers.

Ashley had sued the newspapers for defamation after Internet sites and chatrooms named him as one of the footballers in the story.

The survey was to ask readers if they identified any of the unnamed men in the stories and also ask if readers used the Internet to seek out the identity of the unnamed men.

'There are two reasons I have used the Internet to facilitate a survey,' said his lawyer, Graham Shear. 'Firstly it allows me identity a group of possible witnesses from hopefully a broad base of people. And secondly it has enabled me to do it soon after the publication of articles about which we complained, so that the issues and articles are fresh in people's minds.'

The website also was to ask if readers wrote any blogs about the issues, discussed it with friends or received any texts about it.

Ashley's lawyers also took out an advertising link the website on PinkNews.co.uk, the gay news website that had run stories about the *News of the World* story.

The PinkNews.co.uk editor, Benjamin Cohen, said that the site was carrying a story and an advert linking to the survey because it had been the first to carry the original version of the doctored photograph that the *News of the World* ran to accompany its story.

At around virtually the same time in early 2006, lawyers for the *News of the World* and the *Sun* wrote to websites that they believed named the player following articles in the papers that spoke of high-profile football players being involved in gay sex sessions.

The lawyers wrote to the websites putting them on notice that their publishers, News Group Newspapers, would be seeking an indemnity for any damages and costs they could face should Cole win his case.

Such a move could effectively have spread or even transferred the liability onto the websites that published Cole's name, should he win his case.

A statement issued by the *News of the World* said, 'The

irony of this case is that those who did not identify Cole as being allegedly involved have been sued. Those who did and continue to name him have not.'

The statement added, 'The newspaper's liability ends with its publications and does not extend to subsequent publications by others. Liability for damage caused by website publications lies with the website publishers. This case demonstrates the wider danger of uninhibited publication on the Internet where there is a reckless disregard for the defamation laws of this country.'

Eventually, Ashley and his a radio DJ pal received an apology and damages from the *News of the World* over the articles.

The apology was printed on Page 3 of the *News of the World* on the day of the World Cup clash with Ecuador in Germany and it said:

Although the photograph was pixelated some readers have understood Mr Cole to be one of the footballers and Masterstepz to be the DJ concerned. We are happy to make clear that Mr Cole and Masterstepz were not involved in any such activities. We apologise to them for any distress caused and we will be paying them each a sum in the way of damages.

The newspaper also wished Ashley 'the very best of luck' in the match against Ecuador.

It was a game that England won 1–0 thanks to a David Beckham goal, but England suffered their almost ritual heartache in the next knockout game when they lost in a penalty shootout to Portugal in the quarterfinals. Beckham was injured – he subsequently resigned the captaincy – Rooney red-carded and the World Cup finals came to an end for another four years.

Or, as a clutch of newspaper couldn't resist putting it, THE WAGS PACK THEIR BAGS.

There were lists asking who would take over from Victoria Beckham as top WAG – Coleen narrowly beat Cheryl for that title – and there were even the 'WAG Awards'. Cheryl won the 'biggest sunglasses' category.

Cheryl had often remarked that she did not want to fall into the 'WAG category' and was famously to remark, in the *New Statesman*, of all places, some time later, 'Footballers' wives are just as bad as benefit scroungers. These women have nannies, they don't cook or clean and never do a day's work. What kind of aspiration is that?'

With England out of the tournament she spelt it out again: 'It really annoys me when people try to call me a footballer's wife. Footballers' wives have no careers and live off their husbands' money. You see girls in clubs making a beeline for the footballers and it makes me sick.

'It's like a comedy. Everyone's so flash. It's like, "Who's got the best watch on, who's got the best bag, which wife is dressed the best, which has got the best hair?" I'm like, "I've got my own career." I'll sit back and read the mags. I've got my own money, so if my husband's card gets declined I just whip out mine.

'I love Victoria. She's just so witty and down to earth.

She's from a girl band and she's not a typical footballer's wife. She's very ambitious, so we have a lot in common. The first time I went to an England match to watch Ashley was just so embarrassing. All the other girls were really glammed up, then I walked in with chipped nail polish and wearing a jumper. I looked terrible.

'But Victoria was so welcoming. She wasn't intimidating or starry at all. We had a right laugh together.'

Cheryl did say, however, she thought it 'quite sweet' when she and Ashley were called 'the new Posh and Becks'.

'I was in Girls Aloud before I met Ashley and have my own successful career. I'm not going to quit the band and sit around in the sun all day or go shopping with Ashley's plastic. If I'm going shopping I'll pay with the money I've worked hard for. I would die of embarrassment if I had to resort to taking boyfriend's cards.'

Whether she was a WAG or not, and Cheryl seemed to have avoided many of the reported excesses of the girls, there were more pressing matters that now needed her and Ashley's attention: in less than two weeks they were to be married.

6

THE BIG DAY

Before any wedding there are two major obstacles to be faced and surmounted: the hen night and the stag party.

With the lifestyle that Cheryl and Ashley led, they both were going to have to be a little bit special, and they were. If reports were to be believed, Cheryl's especially was a night to remember. The *Daily Mirror* went so far as to say, 'Girls Aloud star Cheryl Tweedy collapsed in a nightclub during her boozy hen night before the WAGs' wedding of the year.

'The stunning singer, who marries England footballer Ashley Cole today, had been knocking back pink champagne and vodka cocktails into the early hours of yesterday morning.

'She cracked her head on stairs in her fall during a wild night in which Cheryl, 23, and her band-mates danced on the tables.'

After losing her balance, band-mate Nicola Roberts rushed over to hug her after she collapsed and hit her head on a few steps.'

Among the crowd were Cheryl's mother Joan and band-mates Nicola, Nadine Coyle, Sarah Harding and Kimberley Walsh, who organised the evening. On their way out, Cheryl, Kimberley and Nicola performed a rendition of 'I'm Getting Married in the Morning'.

The *Sun*'s 'Bizarre' column, which had followed the career of the girls for years, also said that Cheryl had pushed the boat out. 'Girls Aloud helped Cheryl Tweedy paint the town red with a boozing session on her last night of freedom … At one stage Sarah Harding said: "Let's go somewhere else. It's boring here" and Cheryl replied, "No. I'm staying, it's my party."

'The girls went on partying until 3am. before staggering out of the club. They were so wasted that Nicola didn't even notice she had cut her foot, and Sarah followed behind still swigging champagne,' the paper added.

'Cheryl laughed off a wardrobe malfunction as she fell out of her slinky red dress but as she clambered into a cab, one of the girls had to put a hand over her mouth to stop her being sick. Yuck.'

The *Daily Star* too reckoned it had been a good night, noting in its report of 'a boozy hen night', 'Bride-to-be Cheryl Tweedy's pals made sure they helped her bid a noisy and raucous farewell to life as a single girl … Between them they sank 20 bottles of Laurent Perrier rosé champagne, plus shots of Sputnik vodka, as Cheryl toasted her final night of freedom before her wedding today to football hero Ashley Cole.

'And it could have been even wilder if the mums hadn't been there to keep the loud girls in check. Cheryl, 23, who was landed with a relatively modest bill (for celebs) of £750, looked like a WAG who'd need a hair of the dog in the morning as she tottered out of the club at 2.30am.

'The tipsy lady in red was "helped" out of the hen party by fellow Girls Aloud Nicola Roberts and Kimberley Walsh.'

A source at the club said, 'All the girls were dressed to the nines – Cheryl looked particularly stunning in a bright-red dress. They were all very happy and excited and stuck a good few glasses of bubbly away. It was a really girlie night. They drank pink champagne and regularly hit the dance-floor ... Her group mate Sarah Harding spent the night dancing – even leaping on a table at one stage.'

The *Star* quoted a party insider as saying, 'After about two and a half hours of drinking and dancing the girls decided to call it a night ... Cheryl and the rest of Girls Aloud left by the back door of the club, while her friends and family came out of the front. She looked a little the worse for wear but very happy as she got outside in the fresh air. At one stage Cheryl struggled to prevent a boob from tumbling out when she suffered a wardrobe malfunction.'

Ashley too was making every moment of his last few days of 'freedom' count. He went on a stag do in a trendy part of Spain, although he didn't like that phrase, thinking it inaccurate and saying, 'It was nothing but a break to be honest,' adding, 'I needed to get away. An escape from reality for a bit. I needed to get a clear head for the wedding.'

He flew out to Spain with England pals Jermaine Jenas and some friends and he hit sun-soaked Puerto Banús on the Costa del Sol. Jermaine Jenas seemed to be having the wilder time, with drinking games and frolics with other sun seekers.

The pair were later joined by England and Manchester United defender Rio Ferdinand for the break. Ashley was clearly missing Cheryl, and chatted intently to her on his mobile as he chilled out by the pool in the millionaires' resort near Marbella.

His friends were on hand, however, to help him take his mind of the wedding for a while with a knees-up at Lineker's bar after their first day at the beach. Jenas even took part in a pint-downing contest after watching France beat Portugal in the World Cup semi-final, much to Ashley's amusement.

And later the group were entertained by a glamorous dancer in a private room until 2am.

A source close to the player said, 'Ashley needed a party after the disappointment of the World Cup and the drinks were flowing. There were pretty girls throwing themselves at the players on the beach and in the bars and clubs but Ashley's very much in love with Cheryl and he's used to having to palm off keen girls.'

Ashley was on his best behaviour during the lads' nights out, although Tottenham player Jenas was more than happy to flirt with female fans and join in the drinking game with the DJ. A holidaymaker said, 'Jermaine took his top off and revealed his toned body behind the bar with hundreds of people watching and cheering him on like he was the star of the show.

'He had to down a pint of lager quicker than the DJ but ended up just pouring most of it all over his head – it was hilarious.

'He was covered in beer and everyone was laughing. Ashley was in hysterics, too. A blonde barmaid patted Jenas dry and then he was ordered to wear a Zorro hat and cape. Later the boys took the party upstairs to a private room and a bouncer ensured only those with an invitation got in.'

The nuptials of Cheryl and Ashley – unkindly dubbed 'The C&A Wedding' by some – were attracting massive interest. *OK!* magazine had tied up the ceremony and party to the tune of a reported £1 million, even though years earlier Cheryl had dismissed the idea of ever doing such a deal should she marry.

A 'celebrity wedding' is a very complicated event to arrange, with restrictions most normal couples would never have to worry about. One such meant that guests were asked not to ask any of the attending celebrities for their autographs. The couple also wanted everyone invited to sign a highly restrictive confidentiality agreement before they were allowed to attend.

Cheryl was thought to have made the request because she was apprehensive about the way their friends and family from ordinary backgrounds would react to seeing other guests who are in the public eye – especially during the evening festivities.

One guest who received the invitation was quoted in the *Mail on Sunday* as saying, 'I was really surprised to be told I couldn't ask for anyone's autograph, but it's not the kind of thing I'd do at a wedding anyway. They must be worried that there are some relatives who will go up and badger the England team and any of the players who are there. But it seems a bit much to go to the trouble of putting it in a contract.'

The newspaper contacted Cheryl's representatives, but they did not make any comment about the situation.

Out of necessity the bride- and groom-to-be also made elaborate attempts to keep the wedding plans secret. Invitations sent out the previous month did not even reveal the location of the wedding. Instead, guests were told to ring a special hotline two days before the ceremony to find out where they needed to go. Practically all the media still thought it was going to be at Highclere and were continually referring to it as the venue for Katie Price, also known as Jordan, and her doomed wedding to Peter Andre.

The references to Ashley and Cheryl's being the new Posh and Becks were also inevitable and the comparisons between the two weddings were being made even before Cheryl and Ashley said 'I do'.

The wedding was constantly being discussed in magazines and newspapers, but, in the run-up to the big day, the young couple managed to come up with something that overshadowed even that future great occasion: a photoshoot that was universally dubbed one of the most embarrassing of all time.

'Cheesy' was the word on everyone's lips when Cheryl and Ashley were pictured in front of a white limousine order to promote Camelot's Dream Number launch as part of the National Lottery.

Cheryl wore a sexy thigh-high number from Italian designer Roberto Cavalli, who had designed her wedding dress. But it was Ashley who really caught the eye in his white suit, medallion and jewelled belt. Perhaps it was tongue-in-cheek, in which case it might just have been excusable. If it was meant to be serious, oh dear!

Some of the kinder comparisons were with John Travolta in *Saturday Night Fever*; others said he was a dead ringer for Theophilus P. Wildebeest, the overtly sexy, hopelessly uncool creation of comedian Lenny Henry.

Joan Collins's daughter Tara Newley said in an open letter to Ashley, 'You may look good in an England kit, but hamming it up with Cheryl Tweedy – days before your wedding – in cheesy white outfits to promote the National Lottery earned you a red card for style.'

Such criticisms, coming as they did just days before their wedding, can't have made pleasant reading in the morning newspapers, but at least they had more important matters to concentrate on.

On 14 July, a Friday, the couple had their official marriage ceremony at Sopwell House, near St Albans, a Georgian country house that was once the home of Lord Mountbatten. Delightful a setting as it was, it was hardly the glitz-and-glam affair that the world was expecting from such a high-profile couple. The reason that the marriage took place there was simple: Sopwell House was legally licensed to have marriage ceremonies conducted; Wrotham Park wasn't. The two proud mums, Cheryl's Joan and Ashley's Sue, watched as the registrar carried out the ceremony. The proceedings lasted just 30 minutes and Ashley listed his profession as 'professional footballer' and Cheryl hers as 'recording artist'. The guests then celebrated with champagne and roast-beef sandwiches, although stayed up that evening and had a few more drinks at the hotel he was staying at that night.

It had been a small, family affair with under 30 guests, and carried out in secrecy – unlike what was to follow the next day.

Many news outlets were saying right up until hours before the big Saturday ceremony that the marriage was to be at Highclere, but as the day wore on word leaked out. It wasn't surprising that it had as squads of suited security guards and coachloads of relatives put up the night before in a nearby Travel Inn. There was a blacked-out carriage, too, which was, to put it mildly, not usual at weddings.

The big event saw Ashley nervously rehearsing his speech in his room at the Grove Hotel in Hertfordshire. As tradition demands, he and Cheryl had spent the night apart from each other and Ashley was surrounded by his friends in his bedroom as the minutes ticked by on that Saturday morning. Even though the couple were legally already wed, he was enduring the sort of pre-wedding lull that countless young men have felt before and many will continue to feel for years to come. The Cole entourage watched *Soccer AM* on Sky as the groom began to feel the heat in his white Roberto Cavalli tailcoat. He had a quick glance at the two his-and-hers ring boxes, looking swiftly at Cheryl's large, eight-carat, heart-shaped, yellow diamond with a cluster of smaller stones and a white-gold band by London designer Stephen Webster.

At the same time Cheryl was with her mother and her bridesmaids. She too was in Roberto Cavalli, a satin wedding dress. The bustier shone with diamante, sequins and beads Cheryl, who decided against wearing a veil but did wear a diamond tiara, looked gorgeous in her dress with its soft beaded bow and trailing ribbon effect, created to follow the shape of her body, while the back of the dress flowed into a train that was trimmed with tiny bows and lay on a pillow of silk tulle.

The shape of the dress was inspired by the Ming-vase dress from the designer's autumn/winter 2005 collection. Victoria Beckham had worn a similar version to Elton John's White Tie & Tiara Ball in 2005. Many said her dress was Victoria's influence, but Cheryl insisted, 'There's been loads of speculation that it was Victoria who put me in but it was actually nothing to do with her. We just both love that designer. I just looked through some designs Roberto had sketched and it turned out my favourite was his favourite as well.' Several reports of the wedding said the dress alone cost £110,000.

There had been constant speculation that David and

Victoria Beckham would be guests at the wedding, but they could not be there, although David's mother Sandra, who knew the couple, was. It transpired that the abundance of celebrities who had been mooted as likely to be there did not appear, although Ashley's Arsenal and England team-mate Sol Campbell was among those celebrating.

Cheryl, as well as using Victoria's dress designer, used the same flower arranger, Simon Lycett, and the Little Venice Cake Company, who had baked David's 30th birthday cake.

Food that evening was going to be prepared by Rhubarb Food Design, the upper-crust caterers who had handled Prince Edward's wedding to Sophie Rhys-Jones. The first course was prawn-and-crayfish cocktail, smoked salmon with watercress, a parmesan wafer and lemon wedges accompanied by roasted and grilled vegetables with a pesto dressing. It was followed by fillet steak, chunky chips, grilled mushrooms, peas, grilled tomatoes, onion rings and Madeira jus. It led one newspaper to call it a steak-and-chips affair!

At 5pm Cheryl's father Garry Tweedy led her from her bedroom to the carriage and the white horses waiting to pull it through the grounds of the mansion to the small chapel where Ashley was waiting with the Rev. Keri Eynon and where the couple were to exchange vows. Ashley's mother was to his left with his family; Cheryl's mother and family were to the right. A small gospel choir, seven-strong and wearing white suits, were beneath the stained-glass windows.

Both bride and groom had to make their way into the

chapel through what was by now a throng of cameramen. A tarpaulin had been erected to prevent them getting photographs, one of the elements that went with the territory of doing an exclusive deal with *OK!*.

Cheryl was shielded from the world by an army of minders armed with white sheets. However, two feet in sandals and a touch of the bridal dress peeped out beneath the sheets. A few minutes earlier, the Girls Aloud bridesmaids had arrived in three separate silver Mercedes limousines.

And Cheryl, accompanied by father Garry in a chocolate-brown designer suit, made it into the chapel under what the next day was described as 'a shroud' – again for the purpose of stopping her being photographed. Cheryl's sister Gillian was the maid of honour and her younger brother, Garry junior, was ring-bearer. The page boys were her three nephews and the Girls Aloud members, in Cavelli-designed coral pink dresses, were bridesmaids. They all looked the epitome of a happy, contented English family on one of the happiest days of their life, although it was unfortunate that elder brother Andrew was not able to be among the 50 guests in the chapel, as he was still serving his sentence for the crimes he had carried out in Newcastle.

Ashley later admitted in his biography that he could not stop the tears from flowing as Cheryl walked down the aisle. 'I had a tear in my eye when I first saw her, and then I did cry – I'm not afraid to admit it. She just looked so amazing, like a little princess.'

Cheryl too was affected: 'He wouldn't look at me when

I first saw him and I was thinking, "Why won't you look at me?" Then I saw that he was crying and that just set me off.'

The choir sang 'Ain't No Mountain High Enough' as the couple exchanged vows and the two mothers lit candles. Ashley and Cheryl then used them to light another couple of candles, which symbolised the unity of the two families.

The happy couple walked back down the aisle to the strains of 'Oh Happy Day' and were then were helped back into their horse-drawn carriage beneath white sheets, again to prevent unwanted pictures being taken, and driven back across the lane and into the grounds of Wrotham Park as the day, estimated to have cost over £500,000, continued.

Four minders ran alongside the coach like royal footmen and the rest of the wedding party then climbed into waiting blacked-out Mercedes limousines and were driven to the reception.

The two Rolls-Royces that had earlier delivered Ashley and his best man and ushers then returned to collect other key members of the party, who were also helped in beneath blankets. The relatives and friends of the couple were ferried to the reception by a fleet of blacked-out Chrysler people carriers.

Then it was time for the couple to meet their 250-plus guests, waiting patiently for them inside a vast network of marquees for the meal and the evening's entertainment

Events organiser Julian Poznos, head of the entertainment company Banana Split Events, said, 'The main marquee was lit by beautiful illuminated columns, candles and with rose petals on the tables and there were flowers hanging above the heads of the bride and groom.'

Over £50,000 was spent on the catering by Rhubarb Food Design at £200 per head for the food. And an extra £60,000 was spent on champagne. Poznos added, 'They were served lovely food – prawn-and-lobster cocktails for starter. Steak and chips were the main course washed down with pink champagne.'

As well as the food and drink, there were, naturally enough, the speeches. Garry Tweedy, as all proud fathers are wont to do, paid tribute to his daughter and said, 'When Cheryl was born I thought I was handed an angel. It was the proudest day of my life. She's independent, smart and stunning, perfect in every way. I couldn't ask for a better daughter. What I wanted for her was a smart, sensible, reliable partner and I'm delighted Ashley is all those things and I'm delighted to welcome him into our family.'

Then he brought the house down by suddenly producing a black-and-white-striped Newcastle shirt with Number 3 on the back and the name 'Cole' on it. 'Come on, Ashley, make my dream come true.'

The best man's speech was by Ashley's brother, and, in his own three-minute address to the revellers, Ashley told them, 'I'm the luckiest, happiest man around today and I'm proud to call myself Cheryl's husband and Cheryl as my wife.' He also called her 'my biggest support, my best friend, now my wife'.

As is customary at weddings, the bride and groom were the first on the dance floor. But this was not to be an ordinary number: the revolving stage turned and there, waiting to perform, was one of Ashley's favourites, the American singer John Legend. Ironically, he did not really know too much about the happy couple. Apart from David Beckham, no British soccer stars are known in the States, and Girls Aloud had not made it big in America.

Nevertheless, he said, 'It was a surprise she wanted for him. I thought that was really nice. It was cool. It was a nice vibe at the wedding and they were really sweet and they looked incredible. It was nice to be there.'

After he had finished, the guests, including the Sugarbabes and Jamelia, started dancing as Ashley's pal DJ Masterstepz played some music. There are no bedrooms available at the stately home and it was 2am before Cheryl slipped into her going-away cocktail dress – by Cavalli, of course – and she and Ashley prepared to leave on their honeymoon.

Cheryl had decided that she was going to be known as Cheryl Cole, not Cheryl Tweedy, from thereon and, when *OK!* magazine with its 44 pages on the wedding was published a few days later she also said that she had refused to draw up a prenuptial agreement with Ashley.

Asked if the couple had signed such an agreement, she replied, 'No, I think that's defeating the point. We're getting married because we're committing ourselves to each other to spend the rest of our lives together. No ifs and buts. I think it's disgusting. I could understand if you're 93 and you've got billions of pounds and this 24-year-old wants to marry you in a month. But we're a work in progress, we're going to build our married life together not thinking about if it ever ends.'

The wedding, and its subsequent coverage in *OK!* made it a prime target for those who sneered at the entire 'footballers' wives' phenomenon. 'C & A' were an easy target, and there was no shortage of people willing to take aim and fire.

Marina Hyde in the *Guardian* referred to it as 'yet another Showbiz Wedding of the Year', saying, 'In fairness, it's all there – Cinderella coach, tattooed bridesmaids and an apparent boycott by England players deluded enough to believe themselves above appearing in other people's photoshoots.'

She added that the magazine coverage:

Shakes down to about 837 photos of the happy couple and their non-famous families, and one shot of a tense Sol Campbell. It certainly comes to something when fellow guest Jermaine Pennant has declined to be pictured. In fact, despite having combed the coverage three times, the reference to 'Hollywood superstars' remains cryptic, unless the Hollywood in question is the Romford nightclub of that name.

To take up the slack, Cheryl and Ashley provide a lengthy interview, in which Cheryl breaks her silence to deliver the definitive verdict on England's calamitous World Cup campaign. 'It's not like we went out because of bad football,' she explains. 'It was bad luck and a shit ref.'

Thankfully, this is not the only indication that Cheryl will not permit her self-doubt to prevent her from being an actively involved footballer's wife, at least if the subsequent argument about whether Ashley can wear his ring for games is anything to go by. 'It could hurt someone,' he reasons.

'You could put a plaster over it,' says Cheryl. 'I'm going to suggest that to Arsène Wenger.'

Continuing in the same vein, Hyde wrote, 'Fortunately, Cheryl resisted the decision to ape her new best friend and fly a flag on the day – the takeout image of the Beckhams' wedding is, of course, the pennant fluttering atop the venue, bearing the legend "VD" – and instead plays up the dark side of her luxury stay in Baden-Baden. "To be honest," Cheryl reveals, "I felt a bit like a prisoner in that hotel." Just as well she avoided a spell in Holloway after that incident with the nightclub loo attendant.

With that, all that remains is for the pair to explain to enthralled readers that getting married is like "being suctioned together". Please, no "sectioned, actually" jokes.'

The Times, too, couldn't resist a dig at the clothes the male guests wore.

Tradition dictates that no one should upstage a bride on her wedding day. But there's one exception: the footballer's wedding. Here all guests (and especially the male ones) must dress in the most flamboyant way possible, so as to a) procure a lucrative deal with a glossy magazine; b) ensure an advertising deal with M&S, Burton or Asda; and c) convey the idea that, despite kicking a ball around a field 365 days a year, they are, in fact, interesting people. For the perfect example, see this weekend's nuptials of the 'career WAG' and Girls Aloud member Cheryl Tweedy and the England left-back Ashley Cole, a glittering example of excess, ostentation and *Dynasty*-style glamour, complete with tonnes of hairspray and sequins. And that was just the guests.

Victoria Coren wrote in *The Observer*:

The coverage of Ashley Cole and Cheryl Tweedy's wedding in *OK!* magazine is as delightful as could be expected. Oodles of information about the outfits, the harpists, the rings, the food, the cake … In fact, due to the unfortunate lack of celebrity guests, there is a quite unfeasible amount of information about the outfits, the harpists, the rings, the food, the cake …

Rumour has it that some stars snubbed the day, rather than play an unpaid role in the magazine story. What spoilsports … Ashley Cole's guests had nothing to amuse them but lychee martinis, Duchesse satin, and the Versailles roses in Cheryl's sumptuous bouquet. (Press me on the coverage, and I can tell you where the lychees were grown.)

If this sniping at the wedding and its coverage was upsetting to the bride and groom, they were at least a long way away from all the vitriol: they had headed to the Seychelles for their honeymoon.

7

TRUE BLUE

Ashley Cole was still an Arsenal player when he returned from honeymoon, but that was not to last long.

His move to Chelsea had been an on/off saga for a long time and seemed to have hit another stumbling block when Arsenal sought £30 million for his services, a figure he thought unrealistic.

That problem was solved when the deal was finalised with William Gallas moving to Arsenal while Ashley crossed over with him and went to Chelsea with an extra £5 million being paid by the Stamford Bridge club. That, however, was not the end of the matter.

Many people had compared Cheryl and Ashley to Posh and Becks, but it was never going to be like-for-like. David Beckham was a media-friendly figure who, apart from a fairly constant stream of gentle ribbing, generated a great deal of affection from the public. Ashley, no matter what he did, was just not as user-friendly, and he couldn't be blamed for that.

There was no hiding the fact that a number of fans, no doubt unfairly, failed to gel with the young full-back, even though he was by this time one of the best players in the world in his position.

And if that was reflected in an indifference among football supporters in general, it was accentuated by Arsenal fans in particular. They regarded him as one of their own, because he had been associated with the club since boyhood, coming up through their youth ranks, so his dissatisfaction with his place in the Gunners' setup irked them more than most. That disquiet was soon to explode in a wave of resentment bordering on antagonism when his autobiography *My Defence* was published. His general remarks about how he felt he had not been fairly treated at Arsenal were interpreted by some as a self-pitying lament and one comment in particular was to stay with him long after the book was published.

In Chapter 2 he described how he was driving along the North Circular Road, the A406, towards his mother's house on 19 January 2005, when he took a telephone call. At that moment his agent Jonathan Barnett was in discussion with the then Arsenal vice-chairman David Dein elsewhere over the player's contract and 'I was sitting pretty, turning up the R and B tunes, thinking the deal was all but done at 60 grand a week and I'd be signing on the dotted line within 24 hours, securing my future.'

Barnett then rang him and said that the 'best and final offer' was £55,000.

Ashley, who had thought the deal was about to be finalised, wrote in his book, 'When I heard Jonathan repeat the figure of £55k I nearly swerved off the road. "He is taking the piss Jonathan!" I yelled down the phone.'

He added later, 'I was trembling with anger. I couldn't believe what I'd heard. I suppose it all started to fall apart for me from then on. I'd trusted Mr Dein to push the deal through. Perhaps it was that he couldn't get board approval, I don't know, but to me and Jonathan it was an agreement and it had gone tits up.'

No matter how genuinely aggrieved Ashley was, when the book was published his remarks were seized on by all and sundry as typifying a greedy generation of footballers, young men who thought being offered £55,000 a week – about twice the average *annual* salary for most people – was an insult.

The ramifications of those remarks and the general tone of the book were to linger on, even after his move to Chelsea. His press conference was mainly concerned with football matters, although his dispute with Arsenal was to dominate the headlines when his book was published and serialised.

First the football: 'Before I went to the World Cup I spoke to Arsenal manager Arsène Wenger. He asked me where I would like to go and I told him I would rather concentrate on the World Cup,' Ashley said.

'I was told after the World Cup there were a couple of

clubs interested – Chelsea and Real Madrid – and I'm happy to be here. Two or three days before the transfer window, Chelsea came in with their final bid and I'm here now.

'Chelsea have won the League for two years running and have a great captain in JT [John Terry] as well as a lot of English-based players. They are a very ambitious team with the players they have brought in like Shevchenko and Ballack. Hopefully coming here, I can win more medals and the Champions League.

'The England players made it easier for my decision. I play with JT, Lamps, Wayne, Joe Cole and Shaun, so that did influence my decision a little bit more. My fitness is good. I didn't have the greatest pre-season, I went back a week late. I trained on my own and tried to keep fit. I have played three England games now and a reserve game for Arsenal so I am getting the fitness. Hopefully I can be involved in the next couple of games. I feel good in myself. In the last game I didn't play too well for England but in the games before I felt fit enough and was getting up and down.

'I've won the League twice now so winning the Champions League would be a great achievement.'

But he also addressed the criticism he was now receiving: 'I hope I make it clear in the book that I don't think five grand is nothing. The £55,000 a week being offered was a hell of a lot of money. But I am trying to tell people that obviously I think I'm worth 60k a week and Arsenal were childish in not giving it to me. They can say I was petty not taking what was on offer but, by that stage, it wasn't the money but the principle. I have read Arsenal fans saying,

"He's been there since he was young, he's lost the value of money, he would have played in the youth team for free." Yes, I would have done, but I've grown up. I have to look after myself and my family. I've got to stand up for what I think is right. Some people will think I'm a greedy pig but it is nothing like that.

'It's never been about money. For me it's about respect. If you'd asked me three years ago, I'd have said I was at Arsenal for life. I gave everything to Arsenal when I was there and I was honest when I was there. But you need that to be reciprocated. You always want to be loved and wanted and feel respected. But I don't think I got respect or was held in high regard at Arsenal. It's nothing to do with money, greed or being disloyal. I can look at myself in the mirror and say that I'm not a bad person.'

He admitted his departure from the Gunners was painful. 'Of course it hurts; I had loved Arsenal since I was there as a boy. Last summer I signed a contract extension. But signing another year was not just helping me – it was helping Arsenal as well. I know I'm going to get stick but I stayed at Arsenal last season and I was still getting stick.'

He was at pains not to be critical of manager Arsène Wenger – 'He has been great with me and supportive up to the last minute' – and he added, 'I don't want to get sympathy or change people's views of me. Of course some people are going to like me, some people are going to hate me.

'It seems that all the Arsenal fans have one opinion. I don't want them to change their minds or love me again, but all the problems weren't down only to me.

Hopefully, people can understand that and see what I have gone through.

'This was just something I had to do in my life. People can't begrudge me for wanting a new life, a new challenge.

'It's going to be different walking into the opposite changing room from normal at Stamford Bridge but it's something I am looking forward to.

'Hopefully I can prove to the Chelsea fans I am not here for the wrong reasons but am here to stay and here to play as well as I can for the club. I have come here to win things.'

He added, 'I won't be walking around London in dark glasses but with my head held high. I have got nothing to be ashamed of. I don't want sympathy. I don't want them [Arsenal fans] to love me again but to understand what I have been through.'

Ashley, who was said to be on a £90,000-a-week deal at his new club, added, 'People probably think I am a gobby little shit and I am on the pitch. I just want to win. Off the pitch I am a totally different person. What defines flash? A nice house, nice car, nice watch? Lawyers, stockbrokers get more money than me, but I'm in the public eye. At the end of the day, it's my money, I earned it. I can spend it how I like.'

He even told the *Sun*, 'I need love. I am insecure. I try to keep myself to myself and maybe that affects how I am seen. I am shy and go into my shell. I need to feel wanted, which is one of the reasons it went wrong at Arsenal. It's never been about money. It is about respect.

'I gave everything in my heart to Arsenal and I was honest with them. You want to be loved and wanted. I don't think I got respected or held in high regard.'

He added, 'It's hurt. Arsenal is a club I loved since I was a boy. Now I have moved on and it's made me stronger. Hopefully I can have the same love for Chelsea.

'There will always be something in my heart for Arsenal. But how can I say I support Arsenal when I am at Chelsea?

'I have said exactly what happened. The reason I have done the book is to let people have another opinion. It seems all the Arsenal fans have one opinion but it wasn't all just me.

'People can think that I was going to Chelsea all along but I don't see how. I thought I would be going abroad when I left for the World Cup. It was the manager who mentioned about going to Chelsea. I had my eyes set on abroad but I got married this summer and that changed my ideas.'

A lengthy interview in *The Times* allowed him to expand his views and recall how, during the protracted coverage of his leaving Arsenal and possibly going to Chelsea, he travelled with Arsenal to a game at Stamford Bridge and saw Chelsea fans wave and cheer him. This was during a period when he was being called a Judas by some of his own supporters.

'I do care what people think,' he said, 'and I think most players do need to hear their fans getting behind them. I do have that insecurity, although I am tougher and wiser after the last 18 months.'

He also spoke of his legal action against the *Sun* and the *News of the World* earlier that year when he said, 'Seriously, it was the most ridiculous thing I have ever heard in my life.

'Some stories you read about yourself and it doesn't matter. But then you hear really crazy things. Enough is enough. I had to take a stand. I can laugh about it now and at the time it first came out I could laugh. But it got serious for a while because it was affecting family and friends. My brother was getting in fights over it. I was just getting married and everything else had been going on with Arsenal. I was starting to wonder what else could go wrong.'

It's interesting to note what Cheryl's views on this slur were: 'At first I laughed my head off because the suggestion was so ridiculous. But Ashley wasn't laughing. It wasn't very nice for either of us, but it certainly wasn't a good time for him. But I was there for him when people had a go at him in the street or asked if he was gay. The thing is, the people who say all this negative stuff don't know him at all. He's such a nice, genuine person. He says it doesn't hurt him when stuff is said but deep down I know it must do.

'To be honest it's more devastating for me than it is for him because I love him and I know what he's going through. I don't want to see him hurt.'

Ashley continued, 'I felt a bit nervous coming in the first day but there were all the English lads to make me feel at home. It is going to be hard for me at first coming here from a rival club. I don't want people thinking I have come here for the wrong reasons, for money, when it is not like that. There will always be a bit in my heart which is Arsenal, but it will feel just as sweet winning things for Chelsea. And I believe we can go on to win everything here. That's what this club is about.

'I had some great times at Arsenal and I gave them everything back. I took a lot of stick in the last year but I got on with it, giving my best however difficult it was. I didn't go on strike. I was playing my heart out for the club even when things were going wrong. I would never let down the team and I would have carried on like that.

'But I was ready to move on for all the reasons in the book and I'm really happy to be at Chelsea. I'm 25 and I know I won't regret this move when I am 35 or 65,' he said.

'All people have heard so far is that I demanded this, I demanded that. I want people to be able to make their opinions and not just from what Arsenal say or the newspapers say, which, with respect, is not always right.

'I saw on the Internet Arsenal fans saying, "Boycott the book". I say read it first because you don't know the whole story. They are exactly the people I want to read it. When they have, I hope people can understand why I was so angry, upset and disappointed at how I was treated. How I ended up having to leave the club I joined as nine-year-old kid when I thought I would spend my whole career there.'

It didn't matter how much he protested or explained, there was no escaping the criticism that he now attracted over *My Defence*. Under the headline WHINGEING ALL THE WAY TO THE BANK, the *Daily Mail* was among the first to let rip:

'A tawdry new book by England's Ashley Cole, in which he bitterly complains at being paid only £55,000 a week, sums up the greed, envy and disloyalty that is modern football.' That was just the start. The newspaper continued,

Manners maketh man was the credo of a long-gone, more genteel age. But today, according to England footballer Ashley Cole, the key quality is money. And the more money you have, the more 'respect' you deserve from your fellows – and vice versa.

This is the philosophy he puts forward in his new autobiography, *My Defence*, as the player justified his decision to join Chelsea last month from Arsenal, in one of the most bitter and protracted transfer deals in football history …

As an indictment of the mores and venality of the modern celebrity, the book is utterly damning. Forget literary prizes: if there was an award for the most odious book of the year, 'Cashley' Cole's tome stands as a 300-page recommendation for a shoo-in.

The article, as well as referring to the nickname 'Cashley' that many now gave Ashley, also managed to refer to Cheryl as 'Posh-lite'.

The *Sun*, too, was taking no prisoners:

Ashley Cole's autobiography – a long whinge badly lacking in perspective – is called *My Defence*. But it has as many holes in it as the San Marino defence that conceded 13 goals against Germany last week.

It is a tale of self-justification and mud thrown at old mentors at Arsenal with all the force of an out-of-control silo-sprayer. And never does the England full-back ... admit his own share of responsibility for the most protracted and murkiest transfer in history ...

For ten years, the club Cole supported from boyhood employed its resources to help turn him into a world-class full-back. Under the guidance of Arsène Wenger, he was rewarded with two titles, three FA Cups, over 50 caps and all the financial spin-offs that come with celebrity.

Yes, he was relatively underpaid at £25,000-a-week. But only in the obscenely over-compensated world of football. Things looked up when Arsenal vice-chairman David Dein offered him a rise to £60,000-a-week.

Then came January 13, 2005, when Cole received a phone call from his agent, Jonathan Barnett, saying Arsenal would 'only' go to £55,000. Cole went on: 'I was so incensed. I was trembling with anger.'

On reading this, others will do exactly the same. All those nurses and voluntary workers who commit their lives to the sick and underprivileged.

Poor old Ash ...

The paper added, 'Cole is a decent enough bloke. But he has seriously misjudged the issue. And he has seriously miscalculated the cynicism with which many regard today's footballers.'

Former MP David Mellor, a massive Chelsea fan, wrote in the *Evening Standard*:

Reading extracts from Ashley Cole's memoirs I have reached a settled conclusion. When the history of self-indulgent tosspots comes to be written, our Ash will deserve a chapter to himself.

After wading through the reminiscences of a man Dr Spooner would have delighted in calling a 'shining wit', I feel like a good bath to wash some of the crap off. Cole's principal moan, in his autobiography called *My Defence* published by Headline next week, seems to be that the £60,000-a-week deal he thought he was getting turned out to be a mere £55,000.

And his conclusion tells us all we need to know about this spoilt brat: 'I don't believe the board gave a damn about keeping me. It preferred to haggle over a difference of £5,000' ...

But at least Ash is honest about his awfulness, telling us after the final match at Highbury against Wigan last May that he didn't go out with his team-mates, but, 'got hammered at the Embassy nightclub' with a lot of Chelsea players including John Terry and Joe Cole ... which reminds me of a famous American political jibe: he has all the qualities of a dog, except loyalty.

Mellor added, 'The book shows Cole to be a greedy little creep, totally divorced from the real world ... 'I had stopped seeing money as the root of all evil. But dear old Ash, bless him, has persuaded me it still is.'

The *Daily Star* also put the boot in:

> So much has already been said about Ashley Cole that it seems ridiculous to waste any more space on the money-grabbing, selfish little child. But I couldn't help it.
>
> When you look at how footballers get their money, through the loyalty and hard work of decent fans who pay for their tickets, merchandise and Sky Sports subscription, the England defender's book – which details his reasons for leaving Arsenal – is nothing short of a disgrace.
>
> After bemoaning the fact that Arsenal tried to do him out of £5,000 a week on a new contract, for which he wants our sympathy, he then writes the following: 'Sitting back on holiday in the Indian Ocean with Cheryl, the idea of swapping north for west London did not seem so bad.'
>
> Thank God for that! Ashley's finally happy, the football world can rest easy. No class, no style. Pathetic.

As we have already seen, Premiership footballers are of interest not just to the British public: they are worldwide stars. Their performances on and off the field exert a universal fascination and that helps to explain why an

American-owned news agency, Associated Press Newswires, which supplied 1,700 newspapers and 5,000 television and radio stations in at least 120 countries, saw fit to summarise Ashley's book and the reaction to it as follows:

'Cashley' Cole, as he is dubbed in the papers, is branded as a money-grabbing, poorly educated, spoiled brat who is dishing the dirt on his former team-mates at Arsenal by saying they are lazy, selfish and dominated by a French clique within the team.

Whether he likes it or not, Cole isn't in the same league as Beckham either on the field or in terms of the millions the former England captain has made out of his commercial deals and marriage to one of the Spice Girls ... And his book isn't getting the reaction he expected.

While *My Defence* tries to portray Cole as a misunderstood rising star who has overcome an underprivileged background, the critics ridicule him as a wannabe personality who is making money by blackening the game's reputation.

This upstart is adding to the gloom all for the sake of selling a book. At first sight, it shows promise – the story of a young player who was raised by his single mother after his father had walked out. He joined one of English soccer's most storied clubs and went on to play for England at the World Cup.

Then it starts to go downhill...

In the country credited with inventing soccer,

business has long replaced sport and Cole is just the latest star who seems to put his personal bank balance at the top of his priorities ... Maybe the best way for Cole to improve his image is for no one to buy his book.

Believe it or not, these criticisms represent the tip of the iceberg when it comes to the flak Ashley received for the book, and Arsenal fans even mounted a campaign urging supporters not to buy it.

It is important to remember this antagonism towards Ashley when it comes to assessing the events that were to follow over the next few years, during which the memory of comments such as we have just read lingered on, while Cheryl became more famous, and more loved, by the public.

Such was Cheryl's increasing popularity that it was no surprise that by October that year *OK!* magazine said, 'Having battled her way to the top of the charts with her gal pals Girls Aloud, she's now starting to emerge as the group's biggest star and is making the front pages of every newspaper and magazine in her own right.'

Perhaps the prose is a little bit too reverential. It was *OK!* magazine after all, but they had captured the mood correctly: Cheryl's star was definitely rising in the sky.

'I'm just a normal girl from a single-parent family,' she said. 'I could never forget my background. Never, ever. I'm proud of it because even people from around where I live, I've inspired them.

'I'm happy to be a chav,' she had declared, 'because a chav is someone who's come from nothing but has, by working hard, made money and then got to buy designer labels and nice cars. I saw a programme about chavs and Posh and Becks were in there. So I just thought, if they're chavs, happy days, put me on the list!

'It would just upset me if anyone thought I was the sort of person who lives off my husband. It goes against everything I was brought up to believe in. It would make me really sick to be kept by anyone. Really sick. And I mean it. We're committing ourselves to spend the rest of our lives together, not to say: "But if we do fall out of love, then you have this house, I'll have this one, you have the dog." I think it's disgusting,' she said, explaining further the reason there was no prenuptial agreement.

'I often pay. He lets me. He sometimes doesn't like it, but I insist. There might be a scene but if I get my credit card out he knows he can't stop me!

'I'm not really an argumentative person,' she told the magazine 'I will say if something's p***ing me off and then I'll calm down when I've got it off my chest. When I met Ashley, it all changed and I don't argue with him. I feel a lot calmer. All my friends and family have said I became a different person when I met Ashley, although I haven't noticed it.

'We don't want to be the new Posh and Becks,' she said. 'Ashley just wants to play football and I respect that. I'd like to take him to fashion events with me but he won't come and I don't force him.

'I didn't like the way her world worked. She couldn't even walk down the street without being mobbed. I'm not saying I'm complaining about being famous and I wouldn't say a word against Victoria because I really love her, but I'm just saying that I wouldn't want her life.'

Cheryl was adamant that she wanted a big family because she didn't think marriage 'would be the same if we didn't have kids', adding, 'I'm talking four or five years' time before I have any kids.'

She was having continued success with the band and, a month after Ashley's book released that storm of vitriol against him, the girls released a greatest-hits album, which quickly went to Number 1, giving Cheryl the chance to say, 'I wish they'd stop calling me greedy. They don't even know me or Ashley. He is the kindest, softest, loveliest person. People call me names all the time – but it hurts more when I hear Ashley being called them. It's so far from the person he is. They don't know how much he does for charity, he keeps that private. He even gets offended if I try to pay the bill when we're at a restaurant. The latest I've heard is that we're buying a house in the Seychelles. It's rubbish. We went there for our honeymoon and it was the most boring place ever. It would drive us mad.'

Cheryl had now reached the stage in her career that her views were being sought on a wide variety of subjects and in some of the most surprising places. Perhaps it wasn't too surprising that the *New Musical Express* (*NME*) was an outlet for her opposition to drugs. She had been vocal on the subject before and she did not shirk from criticising the singer Pete Doherty, who had made countless appearances in court on drug-related charges.

'That junkie idiot. The problem I have with him is that I've lost friends to heroin and I just don't get the idea of glorifying it. I think it's disgusting.

'There are enough drug problems going on without him being in the public eye for it and sticking needles in his arm in the press. If he kicks his habit, he'll be a lot more respected.'

Cheryl added later, elsewhere, 'I'm sorry but it's true. I just don't think his picture should be printed. Young kids who are into that kind of music – they'll just see him as a hero. If someone then says, "I've got some smack here," and that kid thinks Pete is a hero and sees him making something of his life ... I think it's disgusting. It's Kate Moss that makes him attractive. I have lost friends to heroin. It's a personal grievance of mine. I couldn't give a shit about Pete Doherty and I don't care if I never see a picture of him again. The worst part of it is, there are people who really want to come off heroin He's had umpteen chances to get off it in rehab but it's clear that he doesn't want to. He just chucks it back in everyone's face.'

A former boyfriend, Jason Mack, had said that Cheryl saved his life after he became hooked on cocaine. 'Some days I'd blow £200 on the stuff and I'd be drinking bottles of Bud from 8am until I crashed out at God knows when,' he revealed. 'But she'd sit with me for hours to talk me out of going out and getting drugs. In a couple of weeks I turned my back on cocaine.'

If the *NME* wasn't too surprising a platform for her, the same could not be said for the *New Statesman*, the highly respected left-wing magazine. Cheryl and the other girls were interviewed by the magazine and she hit the nail on the head when she said, 'Politicians know we get listened to by more young fans than they do. That's why [Tory leader] David Cameron said he fancied me. He was just trying to be cool. I bet he couldn't name a single song of ours. Do I fancy him? No! Politicians should stop trying to be cool and get on with running the country.

'There should be adverts in the breaks during *Coronation Street* spelling it out in bullet points: This is what the Conservatives stand for. This is what Labour stands for,' says Cheryl. 'You know that basically Labour is the working-class and the Conservatives are the really kind of upper-class, and then everything else is ... I have no idea. I only vote Labour because me mam does.

'We are too young to really remember the excitement of Labour getting into power. All we know is what's happening now, which is that [then Prime Minister Tony] Blair equals [then American President] George Bush and the war in Iraq. So you wonder, "Why did he take us to war?" It affects the young more than anyone because they've got to go out into it.'

In early 2007 Ashley and Cheryl, still very much the golden couple, decided to leave their £2 million home in Barnet in north London, a home where vandals had at one stage sprayed graffiti on the front wall.

Their new home was to be a £3.5 million, seven-bedroom mansion in Surrey near the Chelsea training ground at Cobham, with electric wrought-iron gates, a video entry system and CCTV. Inside there was underfloor heating, plasma TV screens in the bathroom and wi-fi broadband. There was also a beautiful staircase with iron railings, limestone flooring, 8-foot walnut doors and a walnut kitchen.

The home was to be the scene of many of the dramas that were set to unfold in the coming years and it's interesting to note a brief line that Cheryl let slip, which eventually made its way into one gossip item about the couple – they were sharing their marital home with Cheryl's mother.

'Ashley doesn't do a thing around the house. Maybe he'll make me the odd cup of tea, but that's it. Luckily my mum lives with us and she'll do lots of stuff.'

She also said that having one's mother in the marital home was 'not too bad. She's up in Newcastle a lot too. We bought her a house and she said that it was too small – that was nice of her!'

Cheryl was constantly in the public eye by now. She appeared in the Comic Relief version of *The Apprentice* in a girls' team of fashion guru Trinny Woodall and businesswoman Karren Brady, as well as actress Maureen Lipman and comic Jo Brand. They were pitted against a side made up of journalist Piers Morgan, TV's Danny Baker, spin doctor Alastair Campbell, actor Ross Kemp and original *Apprentice* winner Tim Campbell.

They each had to raise as much money as possible from operating rides, serving food and flogging tickets to their rich mates. The team with the bigger takings at the end of the day won the task.

Cheryl said, 'It was much worse than the nerves I get before I go on stage because I was completely outside my comfort zone. When I walked in on the first day I felt intimidated. I thought, "What am I doing here with all these people, what the hell am I going to be expected to do?" I knew it was important that we raised lots of money for Comic Relief so I felt a great sense of responsibility.'

Cheryl proved her worth when it came to meeting the challenge, as she persuaded show-business mega-tycoon Simon Cowell and Ashley to part with £25,000 each and called in celebrity pals Take That and McFly to man attractions at the funfair.

'Trinny is a very dominant personality, very strong-minded. People think I am feisty but I seemed quiet by comparison. I was scared she might criticise my clothes, but luckily I escaped.

'She was a pretty impressive negotiator and managed to get a friend of hers to pay £150,000 for a ticket for our funfair. I was speechless. This woman offered the money like it was nothing. People buy a house for that amount.

'With the likes of Piers on the boys' team I thought we would stand no chance so I just started ringing everyone I knew.

'The rest of the band came to help me. I was so grateful when the girls arrived that I threw my arms around them.

'Ashley also came down to help. I got Simon Cowell and [radio presenter and producer] Chris Evans along, too, so I was pretty pleased with myself.'

Cheryl was careful not to use her feminine wiles to charm the tough-talking celebrity businessman Sir Alan Sugar, famous for his 'You're fired' catchphrase. She said, 'I was told it wouldn't be a good idea to flutter my eyelashes at him, so I deliberately avoided that as a tactic. Instead I just tried to be professional.'

Intriguingly, there was a rumour that Cheryl was likely to be snapped up by Simon Cowell as a judge for his new show. All that Cheryl – who, it must be remembered, found fame herself on the reality show *Pop Stars: The Rivals* – would say was, 'I wouldn't become a judge, I don't think I would be qualified. Who am I to judge other people? I know people think I am fiery but I think I'd be too diplomatic. I know what it's like to be on the receiving end of the criticism. I love Simon Cowell, though. I think he has a good heart.'

If ever there was a case of 'watch this space', that Cowell–Cole combination was it.

Cheryl was 'hot', both as a member of Girls Aloud and as performer in her own right by this time. This five-foot-three size six was also one of the country's favourite pin-ups, her fantastic figure and smouldering dark looks captivated her male fans and even the tattoos she had – including a 'Mrs C' one she had specially done for Ashley on the back of her neck – were a subject of much discussion.

Nevertheless, like many women, she found faults with the way she looked. 'I'm not happy with my body. I have to watch my weight and really put myself through it, trying silly diets or doing stupid gym workouts. I don't like my legs, either: they're thick-set and muscular. Nor does it help being really short. Now I shave my legs every couple of days and have my underarms waxed. I was very thin as a teenager. I never had an eating disorder but I think I was a bit depressed. When I joined the band I put on a lot of weight and at one point was 9 stone 7 pounds. Now I have one day a week when I eat whatever I like. Without that luxury, I'd go crazy! I would consider cosmetic surgery if a part of my body was really getting me down.'

There were reports of Ashley's being out on the town without her, although that in itself was no cause for concern: she had her career that would take her away in the evenings, and he was a young man with a lot of friends who, like him, could afford the good things in life.

It is somewhat ironic that, in the light of what was soon to happen, Cheryl even admitted, 'I've been cheated on in the past and, when I was, I gave the blokes a few right and left hooks. If everything was happy at home and my partner had an affair, I'd want to shrivel up and die. Sex with Ashley is more important to me than all the money in the world. Sex makes me happy; money doesn't. And Ashley makes me feel sexy; he's fantastic.

'We definitely want children in the next couple of years but I'm in no rush. I want to enjoy time with him without any responsibilities. Ashley and I talk about it all the time. That's a part of my life I'm really looking forward to.

'At the minute I want to have my career and have fun.

We're a young married couple, we want to go on holidays and do all that first. Kids are a big responsibility. My mam had my brother when she was 17. I know what hard work it is. I want to have fun first but then be young enough to enjoy being young with them.'

By April the girls were getting ready for another tour and they had just finished filming a role in the new *St Trinian's* film.

In case anyone thought that marriage and success had caused Cheryl to lose that Geordie feistiness, they were wrong, however. She had exchanged a number of jibes in the press with the Welsh singer Charlotte Church, she of the 'voice of an angel', but that was nothing to the verbal feud Cheryl was having with Lily Allen.

Cheryl called Allen 'a chick with a dick' on a television show, which cause Allen to respond in a blog, 'Cheryl, if you're reading this, I may not be as pretty as you but at least I write and SING my own songs without the aid of autotune. I must say taking your clothes off, doing sexy dancing and marrying a rich footballer must be very gratifying, your mother must be so proud, stupid bitch.'

Cheryl then hit back, saying, 'Yes, I was bitchy about her but I never mentioned her weight. Quite frankly I couldn't care less if she has a dick or not. I have had enough of her and her big mouth.'

Cheryl also said that in the past her bandmates Nicola Roberts and Sarah Harding had also been hurt by Allen's sharp tongue – as had Ashley. 'Over the last few months she has called Nicola ugly, which I bit my tongue over. She called Sarah vile and my husband horrendous, but seems to have conveniently forgotten all of that.

'I can't stand people who give it but aren't prepared to take it back. If that's the case she should keep her mouth shut instead of feeling sorry for herself. I could go on but I left school a long time ago and have no time for this.

'I'm currently on a big arena tour with the girls singing live each night. Lily, I could find you a spare ticket if you'd like to come and experience what a live arena tour is like … as that's the closest you'll get to it.'

As well as those remarks about the other two girl singers, Cheryl had also been quoted as saying that Paris Hilton was 'abysmal' in a film role, adding, 'She looks like a Barbie doll and there's no substance to her,' and remarking of All Saints, 'They're all mothers, it's time they grew up.'

Justified or not, all those remarks showed that Cheryl was more than capable of looking after herself in any verbal tussle that came her way. Whatever the rights or wrongs of the debate, the war of words with Lily Allen generated acres of coverage in magazines and newspapers.

The *Guardian*, not noted for its coverage of pop-music squabbles, said, 'Here is something depressingly juvenile and unbecoming about all this. We are not talking about the pop equivalent of the epic battles once played out with fire and fabulosity by Joan Crawford and Bette Davis. This is playground cat-fighting among grown women who should be able to see that a bit of unity and sisterhood might in the long term serve them better in an exploitative industry all too ready to divide and rule.'

The *Independent on Sunday* was so wound up by the dispute that it said it had escalated to 'the sort of name-calling you might find in a Vicky Pollard sketch' (a reference to a character in the TV comedy series *Little Britain*).

It was, as they say in boxing, a right good tear-up. Certainly the biggest British pop has experienced since the glory days of the 1990s rivalry between Blur and Oasis. Possibly as big as Britney Spears and Christina Aguilera's war for the affections of Justin Timberlake. The invective was shocking in its ferocity …

All told, it has set a new benchmark for the undignified celebrity spat … The big dispute is also raising some uncomfortable questions. Cole's apparent reference to her rival's weight (the 'chick with a dick' comment) left Allen complaining of feeling 'fat and ugly', and upset noisy campaign groups working in the fertile ground of body-image politics.

The row reached the stage that there had to be attempts to calm things down. A spokesman for Cheryl said she never even uttered the 'chick with a dick' jibe. 'Cheryl did not call Lily Allen fat. She did not call her a "chick with a dick". That was what Gordon Ramsay said, and when you watch the show you'll see that Cheryl simply agreed with it. Lily should understand how the tabloids take things out of context. It has happened to her as well.'

In the middle of all this activity, Ashley had been busy too. Chelsea won the FA Cup and the Carling Cup and reached the semi-final of the Champions League before losing to Liverpool. They were also runners-up to arch-rivals Manchester United in the Premiership.

By the time the couple's anniversary came around the 'footballers' wedding summer' was in full flight.

Of course, the Beckhams had started the mania, but Ashley and Cheryl had kept the bar pretty high, too, with their bash. On one weekend alone in mid-June four of Ashley's England teammates got hitched in sumptuous splendour. Obviously midsummer is a good time for footballers to walk down the aisle as the domestic season had come to an end, but it did seem something of an overdose.

England captain John Terry married childhood sweetheart Toni Poole at Blenheim Palace, arguably the country's most famous stately home. Liverpool's Steven Gerrard was marrying Alex Curran just down the road at Cliveden in Berkshire with the entertainment provided by Enrique Iglesias, the Spanish singer.

Manchester United's Gary Neville was marrying Emma Hadfield at Manchester Cathedral, before heading off to his freshly finished country estate for the reception.

That left England and Manchester United midfield player Michael Carrick's wedding in Leicestershire looking positively low-key – he was spending only £250,000 on the event.

Cheryl and Ashley made it to John Terry's bash, which was on a Friday, but missed the others as they flew to

Spain for the wedding of Ashley's agent. Cheryl was photographed looking sexy as she splashed around in the pool with her hubby and she was displaying what appeared to be a new roses-and-thorns tattoo on her left buttock to add to her collection.

Intriguingly, the *Daily Mirror* wrote,

> Cheryl, 23, looked relaxed and happy sipping sangria in her leopardskin bikini, which showed off tattoos on her back and legs.
> Chelsea star Ashley, 26, later gave his wife a kiss ...

The couple moved on and were soon spotted in Barbados, where they were staying at The Sandy Lane Hotel although even as they enjoyed the laid-back pleasure of the Caribbean, Lily Allen decided to stoke the fires a little bit more when she told the audience from the stage at Glastonbury where she was appearing that she was dedicating her song 'Cheryl Tweedy' to someone 'very unspecial'.

Then Lily changed the words of the B-side number to have a go at Cheryl. And instead of singing 'I wish I looked just like Cheryl Tweedy', she sang: 'I'm glad I don't look like ******g Cheryl Tweedy.'

Even jet-set holidays can't last for ever, and with the new season about to begin, Ashley had to head back to London for training. The summer sun had done Cheryl no harm as, sporting a shorter hairstyle, she looked stunning in a stylish white jacket as she and her husband were spotted leaving the Cipriani restaurant in Mayfair.

Back in the UK Ashley remembered to buy Cheryl an anniversary present, but it left her cold. 'Ashley treated me to a brand-new Bentley recently. It was lovely but I just couldn't accept it. I have my own Mercedes SUV, and I bought that when I thought I'd worked hard enough to deserve it. I don't feel I've done enough to deserve a Bentley. I'm not one of those girls who go out and spend £1,500 on a handbag. At the moment the car is just sitting in our drive waiting to go back the shop,' she said.

Cheryl was by now in a position to assess her first year of married life, which she did when she spoke with the *Sun* while she was promoting the girls' new single

Ashley, she maintained, was being 'pathetic' around the house: 'He rang me one day last week and asked me, "How do I cook Supernoodles?" I couldn't believe it – especially as it says "boil for two minutes" on the front of the packet. I don't know why he likes them – must be for the quickness because he can't be ar*ed to do anything else!

'He's totally pathetic round the house …'

She added, 'I'm not bad at cooking, I give it a go, but I wouldn't say I was good. I also enjoy tidying up, I find it quite therapeutic. And I'd rather sit in bed with a DVD and a takeaway than go out. That's what me and Ashley do most of the time.

'I feel like I've become a bit boring sometimes. I'm a bit weary of going out these days. When I do go out with Ashley, girls throw themselves at him but I just find it funny. I trust him 100 per cent, so I'm not worried about it. Maybe if I was insecure I would, but I'm not.'

She also said that she felt sure Ashley wouldn't cheat on her: 'He wouldn't dare. He knows what I'd do to him! Footballers' lives aren't always that glamorous. They can't go out and party, and once they've been to training they have the afternoons off. So that's why Ashley is always playing those bloody computer games. I much prefer him to be sitting at the computer rather than out gambling or drinking.'

'My marriage and Ashley are my priority now but the girls are a close second. We were in a position where Ashley could have gone to play in Spain but it would have meant me having to leave the band. So we decided as a married couple not to go to Spain, for my benefit.'

She touched on similar themes in an interview with Piers Morgan in *GQ* magazine. Explaining why she hadn't wanted Ashley to go to Spain, she said, 'Ashley was offered a hell of a lot of money to go … the deal was there on the table. I stopped him living his dream playing out there. It made things difficult. I've been through a s**t, horrible relationship before, so I refuse to argue with Ashley. I disagree with him, that's human nature, but I won't get into an abusive relationship again. So there was a lot of disagreement, and there were a lot of tears being shed. He has always told me never to talk about this, but I think people should know.

'Either I'd have had to move out there with him and commute, or give up my career at a time when we'd finally been accepted as a band and it was almost cool to like Girls Aloud. But it would have been equally selfish for him to go there, so there had to be some sort of compromise.

'I almost begged Ashley to sign for Chelsea, not really knowing what that would mean. I know a bit about football, growing up in Newcastle, and I know it would be difficult for a player to go from Newcastle to Sunderland, for instance. But I didn't realise the extent to which moving from Arsenal to Chelsea would cause so much hurt between the two of us, and to Arsenal fans. And for that I do apologise. He wouldn't have got half as much s**t if he had gone there [to Madrid] rather than Chelsea. And I blame myself for a lot of that.

'Looking back, with all the different advice he was getting and me saying, "Don't go abroad", it must have been hard. He went through hell.

'I find what all footballers get paid obscene anyway, I can never get my head around it. But that's the market, it's not Ashley's fault.'

Speaking about her wedding ring, she said, 'That's worth Ashley's heart. It's white gold and yellow diamond, and it's worth a lot of money, yes. But it's a once-in-a-lifetime wedding ring. And anyway, I'm sick to death of feeling guilty about stuff like this.

'I work long hours, why shouldn't I spend my money how the hell I like? Ashley trains for three hours a day, I work a lot harder. And if I can afford the nice things in life then why can't I have them? I liked the ring, so we bought it, big deal.'

Cheryl also reckoned that Ashley had been mistaken to write about almost crashing his car when he was offered £55,000 instead of the £60,000 a week at Arsenal.

'He shouldn't have written it, I told him that. It was a big mistake because it was written out of frustration and anger, and the way the media interpreted it made him sound awful. Ashley got caught up in all the hurt and frustration he was feeling and I agree that saying that stuff about the figures involved and so on was not a good idea.

'I read Ashley's book before it was published and I told him then that he should not put that stuff in about all the money. Because it is a ridiculous amount, whatever he ended up with.'

Cheryl was always very candid in her interviews, perhaps too open on occasions. She once let slip the England star couldn't have sex with her if their pet Chihuahuas were watching – because it put him off.

Asked how she kept the marriage working, she replied, 'It comes naturally. I still get butterflies when I'm going to see Ashley or when he calls me. We both work away a lot, so time together is precious. We make an effort to go out on dates, but I find it difficult to glam up for him as I always look that way for work. Weirdly, Ashley loves it when I don't wear a scrap of makeup and I'm in my tracksuit. He tells me I look gorgeous and I say: "Are you having a laugh?"

'My priority is Ashley. If he gave me an ultimatum about starting a family which he never would, I'd have to go to the girls and work it out. My life revolves around the other four girls. It's not just a job, so I'd have to make time for a baby.'

And the biggest lesson in love that she had learnt was not to put up with mind games. 'One of my ex-boyfriends messed with my head by going cold on me and not returning my calls. It made me feel weak and vulnerable. Men can be very manipulative. I tell my friends to play hard to get, don't call him, don't text him, and he'll come running to you. It works every time!'

Cheryl's advice wasn't always welcomed by Ashley. He'd been injured and thankfully missed a woeful performance by England at Wembley when they lost 3–2 to Croatia, which meant they would not be competing in the following year's European Championships.

She admitted on BBC Radio 1, 'I tell him to get over it and move on because at least now we can go on holiday early. That went down like a lead balloon, but I'm pleased we can go on holiday next summer.

'He's a Chelsea player, so he's got to think about playing for them now and get over England losing.'

The singer could also console herself with the news that an underwear firm's survey had voted her the winner for the 'best boobs in British show business' ahead of Kelly Brook, actress Scarlett Johansson, Charlotte Church and Victoria Beckham.

8

REVELATIONS

As January 2008 drew to a close, the 'fairytale' marriage of Ashley and Cheryl seemed to the outside world to be as strong as ever and it was business as usual for the couple.

Chelsea, under their new coach Avram Grant, had just won through to the final of the Carling Cup after a tough two-leg tie against Everton and would face London rivals Tottenham Hotspur at Wembley. As always they were highly placed in the Premiership and in the hunt in total for four trophies.

Cheryl was busy, too. She and most of the other Girls Aloud were filming a television series in which they had to face and handle a difficult challenge away from their normal routine. This was *The Passions of Girls Aloud*, subsequently premiered on ITV2 in March 2008, and in Cheryl's case it meant going to the mean streets of Los

Angeles to learn street dancing. Everything, outwardly at least, seemed rosy.

And then came the bombshell.

A night out after a Premiership match on 8 December the previous year was to come back to haunt Ashley. The details that were to emerge were sordid and grubby, and would permanently taint the reputation of those involved.

It had been a fairly routine victory for Chelsea that day, Sunderland losing at Stamford Bridge to a headed goal from Andriy Shevchenko and a penalty from Frank Lampard. Much of the talk afterwards was of a forthcoming match in the Champions League and then the long-awaited return to Arsenal for a Premiership match and the inevitable hostility Ashley would face from their supporters.

The night had begun at the GC Club in the West End, an upmarket venue sandwiched between Piccadilly Circus and Chinatown, where Ashley, casually dressed in jeans, T-shirt and, on occasions, with a baseball cap on his head, was drinking with friends and the plan was later to watch the televised Ricky Hatton–Floyd Mayweather fight in Las Vegas. Also in the club were 22-year-old hairdresser Aimee Walton and a friend, who were asked, by a pal of Ashley's, if they wanted to join Ashley and his chums in the VIP area of the club.

Aimee, ironically a Chelsea fan, was to recall, 'Ashley was already drunk and couldn't keep his eyes off me, but he wouldn't come and chat. I knew who he was but have never been that impressed with footballers – we were just enjoying the free drinks. But at the end of the night one of

Ashley's mates just came up to me and said, "Ashley wants you to go home with him."

'He said he'd get a car but my friend was driving so we offered to give him a ride.'

What happened next with Ashley and the girl in the short black dress emerged, predictably enough, in a newspaper report. Six weeks later, on 25 January, the newspaper which broke the story, the *Sun*, quoted Aimee, from Morden, south London, at length, and she told its reporters: 'As we were walking out of the club I asked Ashley about Cheryl but he clammed up. I remember thinking I was going home with a married man and that his wife was one of the most famous singers in the country.

'I asked him if he would get in trouble with Cheryl and he just said, absurdly, "She knows what I do. I just can't get found out."

'I was really shocked by that – it showed he couldn't care less about breaking his marriage vows.

'He just kept saying to me, "Please don't tell anyone, I'll get in so much trouble." Then he started apologising for what he was about to do.

'He slapped my backside so hard his wedding ring left an imprint. He tried to hold my hand but I could feel the ring and felt so bad I pushed it away.'

Ashley sat next to Walton, who had a 19-month-old son at the time, in the rear of her friend's Vauxhall Astra while a friend of his sat in the front passenger seat. Two more of his friends followed in a black cab and they all headed back to north London. Not just *anywhere* in north

London, either, but Princess Manor Park, the luxury development where Ashley and Cheryl both once lived and where they had first met and where one of Ashley's friends had a flat.

Walton continued, 'During the ride he was slurring his words and was a right mess. Then he just threw up everywhere.'

She added, 'His T-shirt was covered in sick and he took it off. I remember being really disturbed by how violently ill he was.'

At the flat the other three men remained downstairs drinking and waiting for the fight to start in the early morning. Ashley went into the downstairs toilet in the flat and got some tissue to wipe the sick off his arm. He said he needed a drink and got some water from the kitchen and then asked the young woman to take him upstairs.

'There was a tiny landing at the top of the stairs with a bedroom on the right and another on the left – he took me into the one on the right. He begged me to tuck him into bed. I was a bit drunk and knew he was married and felt bad because I knew what was going to happen.'

After Walton went to the bathroom she returned to find Ashley sitting on the bed in his boxer shorts and he asked her to lie alongside him and he then began to caress her.

The story up to this point had been tawdry, but, as she recounted it to the *Sun*, it was to get even worse.

'We started having sex but it wasn't long before he said he felt sick again. Then he just rolled over and vomited on the floor, all over the cream carpet. It was disgusting.'

There was more: 'He had some mouthwash, then jumped back into bed. We started having sex again but his mates piled into the room. After they left we finally managed to get going again and tried several positions. Eventually he finished and collapsed on to my chest. He was panting and clearly had a good time.'

The next morning at 7.30, Walton awoke and her friend gave her a lift home.

The paper finished its article by saying, 'The England left back, who was training with Chelsea this week, has since contacted Aimee to apologise for his behaviour.

'But last night Aimee said: "He wanted to go on the pull and he chose me. I just hope Cheryl can see him now for the man he is – a cheat and a liar."'

The next day Walton added more to the scandal with comments aimed at Cheryl's oft-repeated remarks that she would not tolerate infidelity within her marriage. 'Cheryl now knows that her husband has broken his marriage vows and for my part I'm really sorry. But at the end of the day she has already said she would leave him if he cheats so I can't see she has any other choice but to leave him.'

She continued, 'When I met Cole it was clear he had no concerns about cheating on Cheryl and he treated me like a piece of meat. It's time footballers are brought down several pegs and shown that they can't treat women – whether it be their wives or girls they meet in clubs – like worthless sex objects or people who are only there to do the housework and keep their mouths shut.'

She then added some remarks that looked suspiciously as

though they were in response to somewhat 'loaded' questions: 'The attraction for these young girls who fall for them seems to be the money and the glamour. But I bet Cheryl is feeling like all the cash and diamonds in the world can't make up for an unfaithful husband. I just feel so bad for Cheryl. It was obvious that Cole had to cough up to this.'

It was a sensational story and one that, in a single blow, looked as though it would place the marriage under an almost unbearable strain.

The Saturday after publication, Ashley was rested from the Chelsea side for their FA Cup tie against Wigan. Instead he and Cheryl spent part of the day with his lawyer Graham Shear.

A friend was quoted as saying, 'Cheryl wants to work through it. She loves Ashley so much. She's shocked but feels their marriage is worth saving.'

The grim-looking pair went to see Shear in a dark Mercedes driven by Ashley, whose face was partly covered by his hood, while Cheryl pulled a hat low over her face.

Back in Newcastle, Cheryl's brother launched a vicious attack on Aimee. Then still a teenager, Garry, shown a photograph of Aimee, said, 'Is that who he's supposed to have f*****d? She looks like a bewer to me. Mum's in London visiting Cheryl at the moment. She'll see she's OK. I can hardly believe Cole would do this to Cheryl. He's just not like that. I think he's a really canny lad.'

'Bewer' is a word used in the Northeast to describe a woman who is not particularly attractive.

The words were hardly out of his mouth when another

woman decided to speak about Ashley. Glamour model Brooke Healy claimed he had sex with her after a Christmas party just five months after his wedding.

Healy said they met at the Funky Buddha nightclub in Mayfair – the club where there had been the first public 'sighting' of Cheryl and Ashley – during a Christmas night out for the Chelsea team in 2006.

Within minutes of arriving at the club Ashley said to her, 'Are you Brooke? I've heard about you.'

'He kept asking me if I was a good girl. He said he was "kidnapping" me and said to me, "You're mine tonight,"' the former flight attendant told the *Sunday Mirror*.

'We were just chatting and he was making it blatantly obvious he was interested. Everyone could see what was going on. He said to me, "I'm taking you home tonight."'

The England star said that, in order to avoid their being seen together, he would call her when he got outside, and a short while later he did, arranging to meet her at a nearby casino.

At about 3.30am the pair of them went to a house in Surrey owned by one of Cole's friends and they ended up in a spare room.

She was reported as saying, 'He grabbed my head and neck and pulled me towards him. He took my bra off. It was so hot and I was telling him not to pull my hair because I had extensions in.

'He was laughing and saying, "I'm used to it with Cheryl." After we'd had sex we both fell asleep and he put his arm around me, which I hate.'

Healy said that Ashley was cold and standoffish towards her the next morning, adding, 'I've had one-night stands before and I usually don't care, but with him I felt a bit hurt . . . Ashley told me not to tell anyone about what had happened. He told me he'd phone me, but I was pretty certain he never would.'

Three weeks later, Healy – who had been linked with several other soccer stars prior to the story involving Ashley – said she was at the Embassy Club when she was asked to go to a private room at the club by a friend of Ashley's.

'Ashley's friend was saying to me, "You've got to stop this, you're going to get yourself into a lot of trouble if you keep doing this." He said he knew that I was considering selling my story about Ashley, but he insisted Ashley didn't know that he was there to speak to me,' the *Sunday Mirror* quoted her as saying. She also felt she had to share some other thoughts with the paper's readers when she said, 'He was distinctly average down below. And he has such little hands. His body wasn't that toned, either. I couldn't believe it.'

In an earlier interview elsewhere, before the Ashley scandal broke, Healy had said, 'I don't intentionally target footballers – it's just the way it's gone. People might call me a WAG but why date other men if I can date a football star? They're so fit – and they always satisfy you.'

It wasn't just the 'other women' in Ashley's life who were having their say about the Chelsea star. Cheryl, too, was to speak. She chose the *News of the World* to defend her husband and attack Aimee Walton in typically forthright fashion. 'When I married Ashley I made my vows and promised we'd be together for better or worse,' she said. 'This has to be the worst it gets.'

She also said that she had known about Ashley's boozy spree with Aimee Walton, as he had told her within a very short time of its happening – and he had not had sex with her. 'I'm astonished that girl says she felt sorry for me. If she felt so sorry why did she run to the papers to try to ruin my marriage? I hope she's happy with her first designer handbag that she can buy with her dirty money. I've been through an emotional roller coaster but I'm determined to be strong. Ashley's a wonderful husband and we *are* in love. I won't let this woman destroy our marriage.'

She said that the night her husband met Walton at the CC Club he had been downing vodka cocktails. 'When Ashley returned in a state he told me these girls had been invited into the VIP area and then he got really, really drunk. That was totally out of character for him.'

Cheryl said that Ashley told her that 'something happened' but he was so drunk that he could not remember what. She was furious that he'd got in such a state that he had placed himself in that situation and couldn't remember exactly what happened and, seeing the vomit on him, fuming that his friends hadn't looked after him. 'All he could remember is his friends leaving him upstairs with this girl and him being so ill that he was sick and she was putting a bucket under his head, looking after him. His mates had said the girl was going into the kitchen and getting cloths to clean up because he was totally out of it.

They were downstairs watching the fight and thought he'd be fine.

'OK, Ashley was stupid to put himself in such a vulnerable and ridiculous position. But his friends should have protected him. I've seen with my own eyes the way women flirt and try it on with footballers.'

That night Cheryl gave Ashley a yellow card and made him sleep in the spare room. 'It was the worst night of my life. I was angry and I didn't know the full story of what happened.'

And, of Walton's claims that the footballer had drunk so much that he was sick in between their lovemaking, Cheryl stormed, 'That's utter rubbish – I know that for a fact. I know Ashley intimately. When he's under the influence he isn't capable. When I heard what this girl had said I realised she'd made part of the story up. And, to be honest, that has helped me get through this.

'Obviously, I felt sick to the stomach. What woman and wife wouldn't? And to be honest I felt humiliated and crushed that this girl was saying these things and people were believing it.

'Things were made worse when my family and friends started calling and offering support. I had to tell them that Ashley had told me about a drunken night and I'd kept it a secret for nearly two months.

'I'd only told my mum. I adore the girls from the band but I hadn't even told them. It was something that Ashley and I had to get through together.

'We've spent so much time together, talked and sorted

things out. So I was devastated when this girl came up with all this and tried to make out it was something it wasn't.'

Cheryl continued by confirming that she had always said that, should anything happen with another woman, she would leave, and she would have to confront that reality should it be confirmed that something had gone on.

'But the next day I calmed down a bit and then took a few more days to let what he'd said sink in. Ashley isn't a big drinker, I knew that, and I was shocked about the state he was in. It's so not like him. I never really thought it could be the end because we *are* married and I realised there's no point saying your vows then walking out on a whim.'

But Cheryl admitted to the newspaper that, for the first week, she struggled to cope with what Ashley had told her and she couldn't believe that he was unable to remember anything. She continually asked him about it but he kept replying that he could not recall anything.

'As Ashley rarely drinks and is usually so careful, I asked if he thought somebody had put something into one of his drinks. But he said he didn't know. It was like banging my head against a brick wall. I didn't want to eat or sleep, I just felt drained and hurt and scared.'

Cheryl, aware of her past remarks about how if anyone cheated on her they would be 'dead', pointed out that she appreciated that it was Ashley who had come to her first to tell her about what had happened that night.

She said that the pair constantly rowed over the ensuing days. Her mother Joan was there and she confided in her,

Joan having realised that something serious was going on, as she had never seen Cheryl and Ashley row before.

Cheryl realised at that time that she and Ashley would be apart at Christmas because he was playing football in London and she would be in Newcastle and consequently she endured 'a horrible Christmas, it was so raw'. Nevertheless she was determined that the row would not drag over into the New Year and she was over it; and, even though a part of her was angry, things slowly got back to normal.

'We love each other, I adore Ashley and we spent time talking about things.'

When Ashley's agent got in touch with her to say that a woman had contacted the newspapers to say she had taken part in a boozy night with Ashley she thought it was 'some daft girl' and it was only later that she realised it must be the woman from the incident prior to Christmas.

'It made it worse when people claimed I'd kicked Ashley out. That just wasn't true. I'm still hurt and angry but we've been working things through since December and we're now hoping to move forward and rebuild our relationship. And I'm back at work with the band on Monday. I thought the whole matter was already dealt with and now this woman makes these claims ... I know it must be hard being a single mum but that's no excuse to exploit Ashley and potentially ruin our marriage.'

Cheryl, who praised the support she had received from her friends and the rest of the band, concluded by saying, 'I feel like I'm living in a nightmare and I don't know if people will allow me or Ashley to forget it. I hope they do

... I don't want anybody to be angry with Ashley or to judge him – that's my job as his wife.'

It would be hard for this episode in the troubled relationship of Ashley and Cheryl to get any seedier, but it managed to go one step further in a downhill direction when, with the ink still barely dry on Cheryl's remarkably frank interview with the *News of the World*, the *Sun*, its sister paper, quoted Brooke Healy as saying, 'When we were getting down to it I asked him if he had protection because I wasn't on the Pill.

'He said not to worry about it because he was always getting tests at Chelsea and he was clean. He said he didn't do protection and not to worry because everything would be cool. I'd had quite a lot to drink so I took a gamble. Luckily, I didn't get pregnant – but for weeks I was worried I might be.'

A similar scenario emerged in another report in the paper when it said that Aimee Walton had told Ashley that she may be pregnant and he said to her in a telephone call, 'F****** hell! I'm shaking. I'm sorry. S**t!'

When it was suggested that he should have worn a condom he said, 'I don't do that s**t."

She said that she was disgusted with Cheryl's remarks that branded her a gold-digger, adding, 'There are things he did to me that you simply would not forget. At one point his mates burst into the room and had a conversation with him while we were having sex,' the *Sun* quoted Aimee, as saying.

'If Ashley can't remember our encounter, maybe Cheryl

can ask them about it. I regret what happened, but what Cheryl has said is infuriating and, frankly, ridiculous . . . I'm sorry Cheryl has been hurt, but trying to shift the blame from her husband to me is not rational,' she told the *Sun*.

The world had been fascinated by the wedding of Ashley Cole and Cheryl Tweedy 18 months earlier. There seemed to be an equal fascination now with their marriage turmoil. Public opinion, understandably, was with Cheryl and the universal feeling was that she had been let down by her husband.

Although Ashley had been left out of the Chelsea side as the story broke that weekend, his coach Avram Grant was quick to say it was not affecting his performance on the field. 'There's no problem,' he said. 'He's a full professional, he's ready, but I am trying to rotate the players and keep them fresh because we have a lot of games. You can have a player who is injured now because they played too much one or two years ago. You need to keep your body fresh.

'In football you need to choose players not just based on their quality but their character. I say to my players that I test them how they behave on the very good days, whether they still want to learn, whether they still want to focus or if they think they know everything. And also on the very difficult days, do they take responsibility or say everyone else is to blame? And do they learn from this?'

Not surprisingly, Cole was the subject of fans' taunts

when he did reappear in a Chelsea shirt. When Chelsea played against Portsmouth at their Fratton Park ground, the Pompey supporters sang, 'Where's your Cheryl gone?' and 'He's here, he's there, he's shagging everywhere – Ashley Cole,' which was then repeated by the travelling Chelsea fans.

Cheryl, meanwhile, was trying to get on with her work. She linked up with the rest of the band to film the video for 'Can't Speak French'. Ironically, it was an upbeat song and the girls looked great in their satin corsets, but it must have been agonising for Cheryl to have to be so energetic and positive in public.

She looked distraught when she was photographed leaving the shoot in London. Sources close to Girls Aloud told of how she sobbed as she shot the video and she also dropped all promotional work with Girls Aloud while she attempting to deal with her problems.

'She told the girls she can't handle being interrogated about her marriage,' a source said.

Cheryl needed to escape and where better to go than Thailand?

She had been in hiding in an apartment in north London, and rarely going out, having left the home she shared with Ashley; and, with the world agog for news of her every move, she decided to jet off with Nicola Roberts and Kimberley Walsh to ponder exactly where her marriage was going.

A friend of hers confided, 'She has been through the most gut-wrenching time and she needed a break. She had to get away from the twin influences of Ashley and her family. Ashley has been phoning her constantly but she hasn't been taking his calls. Her family are also putting her under pressure of a different kind. They feel that she should just dump him and move on. But the girls in the band have been nonjudgemental, which is exactly what Cheryl needs right now. They have all told her they have her unwavering support whatever she decides.

'She still hasn't decided what she's going to do. It's the biggest decision of her life. She keeps wavering between the idea that she will take him back and they can make it work to believing she will never trust him again.'

The girls were scheduled to be away for 10 days on their holiday, and after that they were to head for America to work on *The Passions of Girls Aloud*. In total it would mean that Cheryl would be out of the country, and therefore away from Ashley, for a month.

A friend said, 'She needs a clean break to decide the next step. And she's starting to keep to her work commitments as much as she can.'

Cheryl's spokesman stressed, 'This is not a trial separation. The TV show in America was a project that's been on the cards for Girls Aloud for a while and it needs to be filmed for its scheduled broadcast at the end of the month.'

By Valentine's Day, 14 February, it had been three weeks since the news of Ashley's misbehaviour had become public. Although Cheryl and the other girls would eat cheesecake as well as the local, spicy Thai food, she still looked thin when spotted outside their £2,000-a-night villa in Phuket.

One holidaymaker was reported to have heard her talking to a friend on the telephone and saying, 'Don't treat me like a victim. I'm not a f***ing victim, I'm a grown woman. People email me, "Poor you, poor thing". F**k. How can I trust my fella again? He's damaged goods. I knew something was wrong when I confronted him about some woman and he made up some shitty excuse rather than deny it outright.'

Maids and private chefs were tending to their requirements, while spa therapists visited regularly to provide daily beauty treatments. There was even a Buddhist 'spiritual guru' to visit the villa and help.

The girls' only outing was their daily walk down to the beach jetty – where they sat and waved at passing fishermen, and Cheryl, who was not wearing her wedding ring, was constantly trying to make sense of the position she had found herself in, crying herself to sleep on occasions.

She had chosen Thailand as a place to escape to as she had often, in happier times, thought of going there with Ashley, but a friend said, 'The girls have had an incredibly low-key holiday as they know Cheryl is mentally exhausted with the breakdown of her marriage. Nicola and Kimberley are trying to encourage her to eat as they believe her weight has plummeted to as little as six stone.

'But she mostly just jumps up from the table after a few mouthfuls and grabs a fag. Because of the stress, Cheryl's chain-smoking her way through 40 a day. The girls have been stirring most days at 10am – when they go and lie by their villa's pool or have a spa treatment.

'Nicola and Kimberley are trying to keep the mood light by playing R&B and dance tracks on their CD player. They have been dancing around Cheryl singing the words to "Umbrella" by Rihanna and "Wishing on a Star" by Beyoncé. Sometimes she joins in, sometimes she just turns away from them with her head in her hands.'

From Thailand the girls flew to Los Angeles for filming and soon, at the other girls' request, she went to the Villa nightclub, where she was photographed wearing a loud pink dress. Later, during their brief stay in LA, they also spent time at the fashionable Mondrian Hotel, where they met American television star Will Luke, who was with his friend Kenny Rufus. Will said that he spotted Cheryl when she was in tears near the reception desk.

The two men were making a reality show called *Parking Lot Pimps*, in which they both try to charm phone numbers out of stunning girls. 'It was about 2am and we'd been filming ourselves chatting up girls all night,' said Will.

'We were about to head home when I saw this beautiful girl who turned out to be Cheryl stood by the reception desk sobbing. She was inconsolable and looked so sad I had to see if she was OK. We found out she and her friends were some band called Girls Aloud but none of us had ever heard of them.

'We just thought they were very cute girls who were very drunk. We all got chatting and when Nicola asked if we wanted to go up to Cheryl's room I just looked at Kenny and said, "Let's roll with it." '

Eventually some of the gang ended up in Cheryl's room and inside the room. Will, who did not know of Cheryl or Ashley, discovered what was wrong. He tried to tell her that everything would be all right and even asked her to go to church with him the next day.

'I was trying to get her to smile and it seemed to work.' Cheryl was more at ease and in a better mood as the night wore on, and on occasions threw her arms around Will and Kenny and said, 'When you come to England you better tell us you're there because we can show you a good night out.'

Cheryl even said she loved Will's bald head and twice kissed it and told him, 'You make me feel so good. You make me feel much better.'

Will continued, 'Soon enough we were talking about all sorts of things like music, books, movies and sport. I sang a gospel song for her and then Cheryl and Nicola sang for me.'

An unofficial video of the innocent party later emerged – hardly surprising, as both groups were making documentaries at the time – and it showed Cheryl trying to capture some happiness at the end of a draining period for her.

On 20 February, Cheryl arrived back in England on a Virgin flight from California for an appearance at the Brit Awards – and a showdown with Ashley. She was pictured at Heathrow Airport, still minus her wedding ring, her eyes hidden behind supersized sunglasses and a baseball cap pulled down over her face. She wore a stony expression as she made her way to a waiting car with bandmates Nicola and Kimberley, and they all headed off to prepare for that evening's Brits ceremony, where Girls Aloud had a nomination for best group. Cheryl looked stunning as usual in a canary-yellow dress and, although the band lost out to Arctic Monkeys, all eyes were on her.

The main news that everyone was seeking was, of course, whether she and Ashley were going to get back together or whether the marriage was over. Reports of what happened after she landed varied.

OK! magazine had practically lived with the couple for two years, doing numerous other features on them as well as covering their wedding, and even *it* was in the dark about what exactly was going on. It reported,

Cheryl Cole has had enough of all the speculation about her marriage and wants to disappear. The singer has asked pals to help her 'completely vanish'. She has also apparently told them she feels as though her cheating husband Ashley, 28, has ripped out her heart and stamped all over it. However, in spite of all the pain she's gone through, Cheryl, 24, is believed to have confided in a friend that she is actually seriously considering giving Ashley a second chance.

If that's really the case – and we're not sure it is just yet – Cheryl won't let him off the hook so easily and will make him beg for forgiveness. 'She is humiliated and needs Ashley to learn to miss her,' a pal is reported to have said. 'She'll go back, but won't rush. Not until he's learned his lesson.'

The coverage of this real-life drama was, to put it mildly, inconsistent. Or, to put it another way, it was a case of 'you pays your money and you takes your choice'. One day there was a suggestion that they would soon be reunited; the next the implication was that the rift was too great to heal.

The *Daily Mirror*, for example, said,

Love cheat Ashley Cole broke down in tears as he begged wife Cheryl's forgiveness at their first meeting in three weeks.

The England and Chelsea defender crumbled and wept as he told her: 'I've learned my lesson.' After spending weeks pointedly avoiding him, the Girls Aloud singer finally turned up at their mansion in Surrey in Thursday, to thrash out their marital problems ... despite her errant husband's tearful confession their reunion only lasted 24 hours. Seemingly determined to make Ashley sweat a little longer Cheryl has left him home alone again ...

Throughout that Wednesday night at the Brits she was frantically texting and was so nervous about her heart-to-heart with Ashley the following day that she cut short the evening ...

One source told the *Mirror*: 'Ashley is willing to do whatever it takes to make Cheryl trust him again.'

The *Daily Mail* report of that eventful trip back to the UK said that the couple had also met for an hour in a hotel room at the nearby Royal Gardens Hotel in Kensington and, during that showdown, 'Cheryl found it hard to look Ashley in the eye without dissolving into tears.'

Even though he asked her to allow him back into her life, Cheryl was not yet at the stage where she could totally forgive and forget.

And so the days turned into weeks as everyone wondered whether the couple would be an item again. Cheryl was continually spotted without her wedding ring and, when she was met at Los Angeles airport by a driver, he was holding up a name card with 'Tweedy' written on it, not 'Cole'. It was hardly an indication that all was well again if she preferred to be recognised by her maiden name.

Cheryl's plight prompted sympathy in the most unexpected places. Lily Allen, as we have seen, had had a running spat with her, but, as the news of the couple's dilemma continued to dominate the headlines, even she was moved to note, 'A couple of years ago if I had read the stuff about Cheryl Cole, about her and Ashley, I'd probably have had a little laugh to myself. But now I actually feel really sorry for her. She's beautiful. That's why I hated her so much. I've seen her in real life but I haven't spoken to her because she'd probably punch me. I've changed, I'm not a nasty person any more. I think I was deeply unhappy before and that's why I was so mean to people.'

The coverage of the couple's relationship was never-ending and it was difficult to say where the truth ended and fiction took over. For example, there was talk of Cheryl's slapping a love ban on Ashley for six months to make him suffer; continuing to refuse to wear his wedding ring; ordering him not to go on boozy benders with his mates; selling the house in Surrey because it held unhappy memories – and also they were to renew their marriage vows. The thinking behind that one was that, though she had stayed true to the original vows, he hadn't. There was also the suggestion that they had sought and undertaken some counselling to work out their problems. Be that true or not, the public nature of their rift left their marriage open to ridicule, and one cruel jibe was that Ashley told the counsellor, 'What's 'er name here claims I don't pay her enough attention.' Yes, it was getting to the stage where they were now the butt of merciless humour, and there was little that they could do to stop it.

Ashley's behaviour caught the public attention to such an extent that he earned himself the dubious title of 'worst celebrity husband' of the year in one poll. He beat Prince Charles into second place, and Tom Cruise and Sven-Göran Eriksson were joint third. Ashley gathered in more votes than all the other contestants combined!

Bookmakers were even quoting odds on how long the couple would stay together: less than six months was the favourite at 2–1; 7–2 was being called for between six months and a year; and odds ranging to 6–1 were offered for over three years.

Cheryl had returned from Los Angeles and was

permanently back in the UK by the end of March. The band were promoting a new chocolate bar aimed at women, Kit Kat Senses, although asking Cheryl any questions about Ashley or the tearful events of the past months was definitely not on the agenda, and any journalists who dared to did so at their own peril.

One didn't need to be a mind reader, however, to understand the possible 'backstory' from Cheryl when she spoke about how the rest of the girls had helped her through tough times. There could be only one thing she was referring to, couldn't there?

She said, 'I often think to myself, if I'm having a sad moment or an angry moment, if I didn't have these four in my life it would be worthless. Everyone's here to help each other. We stabilise each other. Whatever any of us is going through, bad or good, we have each other.'

She described how the close-knit group had been the rock that saved her from despair. 'We don't allow people into our circle very easily because we've been let down in the past. It takes a lot for us to trust people. Growing up I didn't have a group of girlfriends I hung out with every weekend – I had three brothers. So this was all new to me. But I could never have done anything without them.'

And she did refer to that break in Thailand with two of the other girls when she said, 'It was the best girlie holiday. We sunbathed, chatted and drank cocktails.'

The other band members were keen to support her. Nadine Coyle, who was living in Los Angeles, was in constant touch with Cheryl as she fought to cope with

Ashley's actions, and she said, 'We talk and text all the time.'

Kimberley added, 'We've been together so much we're like sisters – and you know what you're like about your sisters. We're very protective of each other. We can say stuff about each other, but no one else can.'

Cheryl even seemed to have remembered how to laugh again when she laughingly said she fancied Ashley's former boss at Chelsea, José Mourinho. 'He's cool. I fancy him because he's dead cocky and arrogant. I've only ever seen him from a distance, though. It's a secret crush ... maybe not any more!'

In the midst of all this marriage on/off mayhem, Cheryl still found time to show her commitment to her hometown of Newcastle when she helped launch a charity setup after the death of a promising young footballer from the area.

She said she was 'honoured' to support the Jordan David Thompson Memorial Fund for Teenage Cancer Trust North East – the Toma Fund (named after Jordan's nickname). She pledged to help raise funds for a new teenage-cancer unit, which was to be built at the Royal Victoria Infirmary (RVI) in Newcastle. Jordan's family set up the Toma Fund in his memory, after the teenager, of West Denton, Newcastle, lost his battle with cancer aged just 15.

Cheryl said, 'Because it's my home town I am honoured to be involved in such a great charity. The new unit at the RVI would be the perfect tribute to Jordan's short life.'

The youngster was signed to Newcastle United's Academy as a boy, and United defender Steven Taylor said,

'I knew Jordan from when he was in the academy and he was a good player. He was always keen to raise funds for the teenage cancer unit when he was still alive. He would be very proud to see what has been set up in his name.'

The exact state of Cheryl and Ashley's marriage was far from clear to the general public. It seemed as though the marriage was 'back on' but on what terms and under what conditions it was difficult, at that stage, to be sure.

However, at the end of April, Ashley's mother Sue let slip, 'I visited the both of them on Friday and they seemed fine. There have been a lot of rumours that they're not living together, which aren't true.' She added, 'I love Cheryl like a daughter, but I'm not going to stand here and slate my son. I love them both very much and I'm glad they are working it out.'

Cheryl too was trying to place her marriage problems in perspective when, as Girls Aloud began a 24-date arena tour in Belfast, she said, 'I feared I would crack up so in the end I stopped reading all the stuff that was being written about me and what was going on. But it's made me realise there are people out there a million times worse off than me. People see me as a role model, but I want them to see I'm human and I make mistakes. I'm not perfect. I want the young girls to learn from my mistakes.'

She even dedicated a song at the gig, 'I'll Stand By You', to those with emotional troubles.

Ashley had troubles on the field, too, as well as the 'Ashleygate' saga at home. Although he was consistently earning praise for his performances, Chelsea ended the season without a trophy, coming second to Manchester United in both the Premiership and the Champions League final, and being beaten by Tottenham Hotspur in the Carling Cup final. For most teams that would amount to a successful season, but the bar at Chelsea, under its billionaire owner Roman Abramovich, had been raised high by José Mourinho's leadership, and many of their fans were bitterly disappointed by the lack of silverware.

While the bookmakers were exploiting the strain in the couple's marriage by quoting odds on how long it would last, Cheryl was also figuring in another of their betting tables.

Sharon Osbourne had announced that she was leaving *The X-Factor*, the immensely popular ITV talent show, and the hunt was on to find her replacement.

Paula Abdul was favourite for the spot, actress Amanda Holden was in the running and singer Sinitta was mentioned too. So were Cat Deeley and Nicky Chapman. Victoria Beckham and Charlotte Church, too, were among those said to be in with a chance of becoming one of the judges. So was Mel B – Melanie Brown – one of the Spice Girls. The list seemed practically endless. And if anyone popped down to the nearest William Hill betting shop in early June they would have been able to get odds of 16–1 on Cheryl's becoming the new judge on the show.

It would have been a good bet.

For years Cheryl had been called, in turn, a girl-band member, a singer, a beauty, a WAG and a betrayed wife.

Now, although even she probably didn't realise it, she was on the verge of becoming known by a completely new title.

Cheryl Cole was about to become 'the Nation's Sweetheart'.

9

THE CHERYL
FACTOR

Simon Cowell did not have a reputation as being acid-tongued without reason. The pop mogul had made a fortune, and was getting richer by the minute, by telling it like it is – or at least as he saw it. In August 2003 he had made a typically brusque comment about a manufactured girl group in general, and one of their members in particular. 'I think the Geordie girl is terrible. I saw her last audition. She didn't sing a note in tune.' This was his verdict on the act he had seen. The band was Girls Aloud – the 'Geordie girl' was Cheryl Ann Cole.

Oh, how times change! Five years later, Cowell was to be one of the main players who helped elevate Cheryl to a level of fame and popularity no one could have anticipated. He even suggested that perhaps he hadn't made that bitchy remark after all, although it had been widely reported at the time.

Cheryl's opportunity arose after Sharon Osbourne, wife of veteran heavy-metal rocker Ozzy Osbourne, a.k.a. 'the Prince of Darkness', decided to leave the show. As she put it, 'It's just time to move on. I love the show, I love everybody there, the producers, Simon. But it's just time to move on.'

She went on to say, 'I've heard that they're asking certain people [to be the new judge]. I think they're asking Cheryl, who I love. They're asking Mel B. It'll be interesting, it'll take the show to a different place, it'll be probably even better than it has been, if that's possible.' When asked if there was one person she would prefer, she said, 'I think Cheryl.'

Osbourne, who said her time on the show had been 'the best four years of my life', added, 'I was negotiating and I asked for a ridiculous amount of money and they offered me an obscene amount of money and it just doesn't change the way I feel. I think I've done my best and that's it.'

Asked whether ridiculous was more than obscene or obscene more than ridiculous, she said, 'It's all ridiculous in this industry, we're all bloody overpaid. We all get paid too much that's why we're all drama queens.'

The Press Association is an organisation little known to the general public, but it is a major supplier of news and features to national and local newspapers, television and radio stations. One 10 June 2008 it transmitted a story which began:

Cheryl Cole will replace Sharon Osbourne as a judge

on *The X Factor*, ITV said today. The Girls Aloud star had been tipped as favourite to join Simon Cowell, Louis Walsh and Dannii Minogue on the judging panel since Osbourne's dramatic exit last week.

Cole, 24, who was catapulted to fame on reality TV show *Popstars: The Rivals*, said it was 'scary' to be joining the ITV1 show.

Osbourne, 55, who announced she was quitting on Friday, has denied she walked out because TV bosses would not meet her pay demands and over conflict with Minogue. She had backed Cole as her favourite to take over her role, one of the biggest on TV.

Cheryl was thrilled and said, 'I'm so excited to be part of such a great show and, although it's scary joining a huge programme like *The X Factor*, it's a massive honour to be following in the footsteps of Sharon Osbourne. The rest of the girls have said they're right behind me, which is really important for me as it will be weird to be on the other side of the fence this time. So, whilst we get started on the next album, it will be brilliant to be a judge on *The X Factor*.

Two of the men behind the show enthused about Cheryl. John Kaye Cooper, ITV's controller of entertainment, said, 'Cheryl is not only an amazingly successful, sassy and talented woman but through her winning *Popstars: The Rivals* has been through similar experiences to those hopefuls who want to take the *X Factor* crown. We're delighted that she has joined the channel that discovered her and look forward to her becoming an important part of the X *Factor* team.'

Richard Holloway, head of entertainment at Talkback Thames, said, 'I'm delighted that one of Britain's most successful recording artists of the last decade has joined Britain's favourite entertainment show.'

One of the other judges, Dannii Minogue, joined in to welcome the new girl: 'I am absolutely thrilled. I called Cheryl as soon as I heard this morning to congratulate her. It's great. I can't wait to join the other judges on Thursday.'

The newspapers, always keen to jack up any form of story about rows on popular television programmes, took great interest in any potential rivalry between the two female members of the judging panel, Cheryl and the older Dannii.

Cheryl started the filming of the London auditions that week and soon the effect of watching a succession of youngsters who dreamed of stardom had an effect on her: she was moved to tears by the hard-luck stories of pop wannabes.

A show source admitted, 'Cheryl has found it hard going. She thought the auditions were going to be a laugh. But when wannabes come on with their life stories it can get quite harrowing. Cheryl has sat there crying quite a lot. It really reminds her of her own background and start in music. She came from a humble home in Newcastle and had to battle to get through *Popstars: The Rivals*.'

It was the same story at the Birmingham auditions: 'Cheryl has such a big heart. She's been touched by the courage and determination from some of the people auditioning. Poor Louis and Simon keep having to hand her tissues,' one of the production staff on the show said.

Her impact on the show was already so great that even her fellow judges were taken aback. Pop impresario Louis Walsh went so far as to say that she was 'totally stealing the show': 'We've only been filming a few days but already you can see Cheryl is completely claiming the limelight from Dannii. She's brilliant on it and just calls things as she sees it. She has such a strong personality,' he said. 'Cheryl also started off on a very similar show, given that she was one of the winners of *Popstars: The Rivals*, so she knows exactly how the people auditioning feel as well.

'Cheryl has brought a new flavour to the show. She's fresh and young, she knows a lot about music, she's opinionated, she's a Geordie, and has had 17 Top Ten hits. So, yes, she's certainly going to be a great addition to the show.'

All the judges had a group of acts they mentored in the later stages of the show and Walsh reckoned Cheryl could come out as the winning judge. 'Dannii won it last year, Simon's won it, I've won it – but Cheryl will probably win it this year. She's going to be sensational and people love her. So I wouldn't be surprised if they got right behind Cheryl and got her *X Factor* career off to a flier.'

The schedule that Cheryl now found herself having to cope with meant that her earlier reaction to England's failure to make the European Championship finals – relief that at least she and Ashley could have a long summer break – had been overtaken by events.

It did not stop them managing a few days together in the sun just a few hours' flight from home, however. On 21 June, the happy couple were seen together and smiling for the first time in months, at Puerto Banús on the Costa del Sol in Spain. It was the same area that Ashley had been to for a few days of R and R two years earlier prior to the wedding, but this time he didn't have his football pals beside him and there were no public beer-drinking contests, either.

Cheryl was laughing and joking with him as they walked along the beach, the first time the couple had been photographed smiling together since lurid stories about Ashley had surfaced six months earlier. An onlooker said, 'Cheryl looked stunning in her zebra-print swimsuit and straw hat. She and Ashley looked really happy together.'

Ashley had spared no expense on the trip and they even took separate flights to try to keep their getaway as secret as possible. The couple had rented a villa and every day he left her sunbathing while he ran errands on her behalf.

The new *X Factor* series was being launched in August and Cheryl was ready to come under the glare of publicity by then about her talent, the show and, of course, her marriage. On the eve of the show she said, 'I know my limits and am realistic about my ability. I would never attempt a Whitney or a Mariah song. You'll always get compared. And there is no comparison.' Asked about audition tips, she replied, 'I would stick to something simple but beautiful,' adding, 'I've been in their shoes, I know how much the nerves and the amount of pressure you're under can affect you, your performance and even your ability.'

Cheryl also admitted it was strange to be alongside fellow judge Louis Walsh, who sat in judgement on *Pop Stars: The Rivals* all those years earlier. She said, 'It's strange to be working with Louis. Who would have thought six years on I'd be sitting next to him doing the same job? I was a bit apprehensive. But he was the first to come to my dressing room. He helped to make me feel welcome.' Cheryl didn't even feel comfortable with being described as a 'judge'. It wasn't a word she felt at ease with. 'I like to think I'm there to give opinion and advice.'

Those stories about her being moved to tears at auditions proved to be true too. She had, as Simon Cowell put it, 'cried like a baby' when she met a face from the past, being overcome with emotion as contestant Nikk Magor sang for the panel in the first programme of the series.

Nikk had been a contestant with Cheryl on *Popstars: The Rivals* and, while she went on to superstardom, Nikk never made it. He was, at that time, singing in between bingo games in Northern workingmen's clubs.

When he sang on *The X Factor*, the judges weren't impressed. And, knowing Nikk was about to be rejected, Cheryl left the judges' desk, saying, 'I can't do this.' She was later seen bawling her eyes out. The reason for her tears was obvious. 'To see someone like Nikk, who's struggled for eight years – I can't imagine how he must feel as this could be his last shot.'

At the press launch of the show there were, naturally, questions about her marriage but she refused to be drawn into talking about Ashley's behaviour, and said, 'Do you know what? I've actually had, in a way, a really fantastic year. It's probably one of the best years I've ever had, ironically. We did the sell-out tour, which was an unbelievable experience. We played the O2 – you can't describe that feeling.'

When Cheryl, who was not wearing her wedding ring at the launch, was asked about Ashley, she replied, 'Nice try, anyway.' She was prepared to talk about Simon Cowell, though, saying, 'Do you know, I have always had a little soft spot for him, if I am totally honest. But I do tell him when I think he's wrong because he's not always right. Just being around Simon, and his ego, he's taught me quite a lot. He's made me a lot more confident and comfortable.'

When asked about her, Cowell said, 'I'm going to really embarrass her now. But she is one of the best people I've ever worked with.'

Cheryl also played down rumours of rivalry between her and fellow judge Dannii Minogue. She said, 'I happen to think women in their thirties are at their most attractive, at their peak, at their most confident and more sexy. It's quite embarrassing that people keep saying, "Oh Cheryl's younger." Having those ten years probably means she's got more wisdom and more life experience.'

And she also dismissed claims that her fellow bandmates had been jealous of her high-profile job: 'If there was that kind of feeling in the band we wouldn't be here. It's just not like that. We support each other and we're all doing individual things anyway. They were actually the ones that almost forced me into doing it. It was quite a tough decision given my past.'

Left: Ashley and Cheryl out in Germany for the World Cup.

Below: Fancy dress for the National Lottery.

Getty

Cheryl showed off her ring again after reconciling with Ashley in 2008 but, *inset*, there were no shortage of hopefuls.   *Rex*

Top: The Girls Aloud on Paul O'Grady's show. *Rex*

Bottom left: The couple out to help open a new shop. *Big Pictures*

Bottom right: The house that Cheryl and Ashley shared. *Rex*

Girls Aloud arriving at the Brit Awards in 2009.   *Rex*

X Factor judge Cheryl and winner Alexandra Burke.   *Rex*

Inset: Cheryl even has her own cut-out doll.

Rex/Mel Elliott, thingswelove.co.uk

Happy times for the couple.

Rex

Top: Cheryl's mum, Joan.

Bottom: Determined Cheryl performing at the Brit Awards in February 2010.

Rex

Returning to England at the end of February as, *inset,* the story of the split breaks.

Rex/Mirrorpix

HE'S LIKE A STRANGER TO ME NOW

Cheryl can't face going back to Ashley

Cheryl showed her sense of humour was as active as it had always been, noting about Madonna, 'She shouldn't hang up her boots, but maybe tone it down. Especially around the crotch area.'

The judges had sat through six mass auditions of nearly 100,000 people for the fifth series of the show – which featured the usual mixture of sublime talent and deluded hopefuls. No wonder Cheryl said, 'I went home and I cried every night. It's a roller coaster. You take on their feelings, really. By the end of the day, you're mentally drained. You can't switch off at all. You're thinking, "Did we choose the right person?" I'd go home and tell my mother what had happened during the day or what was exciting or what was upsetting.'

All that work, and the emotional toll it took on Cheryl, appeared justified when, a few days after the first programme in the series was aired at the end of August 2008, the viewing figures were revealed, and Cheryl had helped it to draw an average of 10.2 million viewers. At one point, the audience hit 12.1 million, making it the most popular X Factor launch ever.

The contest captured 54 per cent of the total television audience on Saturday night, easily beating the BBC's National Lottery show, which managed only 3.6 million.

And it almost turned into the Cheryl Cole Show, with programme makers focusing on the singer throughout. The ITV2 spin-off show Xtra Factor, with new host Holly Willoughby, pulled in an average of 1.2 million, peaking at 1.5 million. An X Factor insider said, 'This was the biggest and best launch the show has ever had. It pulled in record ratings and should continue throughout the series.'

Viewers also saw Cheryl's original audition for *Popstars*, the show that formed Girls Aloud in 2002, and she told *Xtra Factor*, 'I don't know how I got in the band. I can't watch my auditions.'

Cheryl's reactions to the acts she saw were soon captivating viewers. Joseph Chukukere, 22, had her swooning even before he started singing. Cheryl had previously admitted being smitten by a contestant saying, 'There was one particularly good-looking guy, although maybe it was me doing the flirting.' But she did not name him. When Chukukere was introduced to the judges as she gasped, 'Oh my God, you are gorgeous!'

After he sang his version of 'Ain't No Sunshine', Dannii Minogue said to him about Cheryl, 'I think you've got a definite yes from her.'

And when Chukukere, from Sheffield, left the stage, Minogue pretended to fan her fellow judge to cool her down. Simon Cowell commented that she looked at him the way 'a dog looks at a can of food when it's hungry'. Show host Dermot O'Leary joked, 'He looks like Ashley Cole. Cheryl's in trouble!'

The singer's girlfriend was moved to remark, 'I don't blame her for liking him – he's a good-looking guy. But he's taken and spoken for. We're in love and have been going out for a year. Cheryl can keep her hands to herself.'

Not all of Cheryl's responses were of such an uplifting nature. Quite often she was overcome with emotion at the stories she heard. Father of three Daniel Evans sang Barry Manilow's 'Sometimes When We Touch' and revealed that his wife Jacqueline had died after giving birth to their daughter Ana-Marie. Cheryl and Dannii Minogue were in tears as he spoke and asked why he was auditioning. Essex-born Daniel, said, 'It was the wish of my wife. Last year after giving birth to my beautiful baby girl she passed away and I realised life is too short, so I decided to go for it. At least I can say I tried.'

An emotional Cheryl said afterwards, 'I can see why your wife wanted you to audition. I think she'd be very proud.' She added, 'It felt like he was singing that to his wife.'

Evans later said, 'Jacqueline had always been my biggest fan. We always watched *The X Factor* at our home in Spain and every year she said, "You should enter that." But it was never the right time. But if the last year has taught me anything it's to live life to the full. When I sang I knew she was in there with me. She's always there beside me."

Cheryl also burst into tears after hearing of another contestant's heartache. Millions watched as the singer hugged 18-year-old Amy Connelly after she sang a song to the mother she lost to breast cancer when she was aged seven. 'The experience of losing her has given me the oomph to go out and do this,' said Amy. Before singing the Faith Hill ballad 'You'll Be', she also praised her father, David. Cheryl beckoned Amy over and said, 'You've been through a lot, but I totally believed your performance. You were amazing.'

Cheryl really had captured the hearts of the nation and she was now the star of Saturday nights. It wasn't just the tabloid newspapers who were desperate for any news of her: the so-called heavy newspapers were entranced, too.

Sarah Sands, writing in the *Independent on Sunday* and noting her teenage son's interest in Cheryl, felt compelled to comment:

Cheryl Cole is probably the hottest woman in Britain today. Her appearance at the London Fashion shows, in Jean-Paul Gaultier, eclipsed all the professional models. Her forthcoming autobiography (she is 25) will probably outsell even Jordan's. She is a television presenter and a stateswoman for WAGs. She has been voted Best-Looking Girl in Newcastle and Most Attractive Girl at the MetroCentre. Now she is Best-Looking Woman on the *X Factor* panel. Dannii Minogue has learnt, along with Anni-Frid of Abba and Drew Barrymore in *Charlie's Angels*, how diminishing it is to be the less pretty one. It is why women go mad in Hollywood ...

Cheryl Cole has been on an emotional journey, which is what has propelled her from being a so-so singer to a cultural icon. As often happens when women are cheated on, she became blazingly beautiful once her husband, the footballer Ashley Cole, had sex with a glamour model in between throwing up in the car and on the carpet. Like the late Princess of Wales, Cheryl Cole took revenge in her wardrobe. Every time a man sighs that she is very, very hot, he is beating Ashley Cole over the head.

Cheryl, coached by the Diana Vreeland of contemporary style, Victoria Beckham, has triumphed. Her fame and glory will soon eclipse her husband's ...

The *Observer* devoted a lengthy piece on its prestigious 'Essay Page' to her under the headline CHERYL COLE – THE NATION'S NEW SWEETHEART: 'With her disarming compassion and sensitivity, the Girls Aloud singer – and wife of footballer Ashley Cole – has won new fans as a judge on Simon Cowell's show *The X Factor*, bringing her career full circle in the process.'

The article went on at great length not merely to praise her from the rooftops, but practically from the summit of Mount Everest. It would be impossible to reproduce it in its entirety, such was its length, but here are a few snippets.

During the auditioning process, she was empathetic and warm to the point of a perpetual, lip-wobbling teariness. 'You sound like you've been through a lot,' she said to one pretty blonde teenager whose mother had passed away. When Daniel, 38, revealed his late wife had urged him to try out for the programme before she died, Cole's tears glistened fetchingly on her beautifully bronzed cheekbones. She cried. We cried. But she looked prettier than us when she did it ...

Now, every Saturday evening, Cole appears in our living rooms as a radiant vision of dimples, sequins and white teeth. When asked to comment on the contestants' performances, she is both forthright and sensitive, a winning combination of feistiness and femininity.

The (predominantly female) editorial team at *Grazia* magazine recently admitted they had a 'style crush' on her. David Cameron once named her as his favourite member of Girls Aloud. Even [journalist] Julie Burchill calls her 'a dignified, level-headed and compassionate national treasure'.

It is true that there is an unintimidating quality to Cole's beauty, a sense that she is not entirely sure of herself, even now. Regular Cole-watchers point out that during live performances, there is often a slight tremor to her voice when she starts singing as she tries to get her nerves under control.

Cole appears to possess a wisdom beyond her years ... She has long been aware that there is a sell-by date to her own celebrity. Girls Aloud will not last forever and she has spoken publicly of her desire to have children. In the meantime, Cowell (who fondly calls his newest protégée 'the Kid') is reported to have offered Cole a 100 per cent pay rise to return for the next series of *The X Factor*.

Manufacturers of waterproof mascara the world over must fervently be hoping that she says yes.

It was a remarkable accolade for Cheryl, coming as it did not from some celebrity-fixated supermarket magazine, but from a newspaper founded in 1791, the oldest Sunday newspaper in the world.

Male writers were also spellbound. Tony Parsons in the *Daily Mirror* wrote continually about Cheryl.

Cheryl Cole is so great on *X Factor* because you know that every teardrop she sheds is genuine. Cheryl cries not because of sob stories, but for real stories, like Amy Connolly, the girl who lost her mum to breast cancer when she was just seven.

Dannii Minogue is being left behind by the Girls Aloud star not because she is older or because she has had fewer hit records. But because she sits there dry-eyed while Cheryl gently weeps.

A week later he wrote about her again:

Some critics whine that Cheryl Cole cries at 'sob stories'. But if a contestant's mother died of breast cancer when she was a little girl, that is hardly a sob story. And if another contestant's wife died giving birth, that is hardly a sob story. Cole cries at true stories.

Beyond the glamour and the glitz, Cheryl's brought some honesty and unashamed emotion to Saturday night TV. That is why she is suddenly the nation's sweetheart, and worth every million that Simon pays to keep her.

Consuming yet more tons of newsprint in another article sometime later, Parsons continued in the same, almost salivating, mode:

Cheryl Cole's tattoo continues to mystify and amaze me. Posing for a shoot to promote the latest Girls Aloud single, Cheryl proudly displays the barbed-wire and plant-life design that garishly adorns the top of her right thigh.

How can she ever have thought this desecration of her lovely leg was a good idea? Here is the woman with the face of an angel and the body of a goddess. And she decides that what she really needs is a tattoo that belongs on a lobotomised biker.

What I can't understand is that Cheryl Cole seems to believe that this tattoo adds to her allure. When it kills it. Do women think that tattoos turn men on? For most of us they're even worse than fake breasts. Every time I see Cheryl's tattoo I feel my skin crawl at this senseless act of self-mutilation. It's like drawing a Hitler moustache on the face of the Mona Lisa.

He couldn't resist yet another description of her impact when he wrote,

Mocking the afflicted will always be an integral part of Cowell-land and the judges are not exempt. As long as Cheryl Cole (25, married, gorgeous) sits next to Dannii Minogue (37, single, quite nice, er, in a certain light and after a tinny of Foster's) they will be compared.

As the two female judges turned up for the first round of *X Factor* auditions, it was clear that this will never truly be a 'battle of the babes' because the war is so one-sided. Cheryl looked effortlessly glam. Kylie's sister looked horribly glum.

If Mr Parsons' fascination bordered on the obsessive, albeit in a professional sense, women writers too – often the harshest critics of all – were also genuflecting in Cheryl's direction. Writing in the same newspaper, columnist Sue Carroll said,

> Cheryl really didn't have to do much to expunge the memory of previous judge Sharon Osbourne except show a bit of genuine emotion – when you've sat through bum-numbing auditions for weeks on end that's hard to do. But it's precisely because she doesn't manufacture the tears and sympathy that we love Cheryl.
>
> She's one of us and I say that not because she's a fellow Geordie, but because there isn't a cynical bone in her beautiful body. So why a million pounds? Simon would call it the X Factor. And I'd agree.'

Novelist Kathy Lette's view was,

> She cries so much I'm worried there's going to be an imminent shortage of waterproof mascara in the Greater London area. I'm beginning to think she's been taken hostage by her hormones. I think she fulfils the fantasy that a lot of men have about women

– that they are emotional, gentle and they pour oil on troubled waters.

There was more. Anila Baig in the *Sun* wrote,

> To be honest, I never really warmed to Cheryl Cole. I thought she was hard-faced despite her groomed, sparkly appearance. Also, I never forgave her for beating up that toilet attendant years ago. While people fell over themselves to declare the Girls Aloud singer 'gorgeous', 'stunning', 'beautiful', I thought she didn't really deserve credit for that.
>
> Yes, she has a face so ridiculously pretty it makes a mockery of the phrase 'beauty is in the eye of the beholder', but so what?
>
> Just because she had the good fortune to have been spared a beating by the ugly stick, it doesn't make her a contender for Woman of the Year, does it? Cheryl is also mouthy. She was said to have pushed Lily Allen over the edge by calling her a 'chick with a d***'.
>
> She married a footballer, Chelsea's Ashley Cole, and complained about WAGs. She said she would never forgive her husband if he ever cheated on her. Lo and behold, despite her great beauty, he did – and, surprise, surprise, she took him back.
>
> Thus, it was with some trepidation that I greeted the news of her joining *X Factor*. *X Factor*? More like *Vex Factor*, I thought. But I was wrong … it turns out Cheryl Cole, although not a sweetie, is actually

like a cough sweetie – hard on the outside but soft on the inside.

Thanks to her, the so-called sob stories have really been living up to their name. She's cuddled motherless contestants and hugged burly widowers. Her tears have made her a splash hit. She will no doubt earn herself millions by getting snapped up for next year's series – and this has taught me an important lesson. When in doubt, cry.

The country's top publicist Max Clifford was another admirer, saying her popularity was a consequence of both her credibility and her sincerity. 'She knows her subject because, professionally, she does exactly what she's judging. At the same time, she comes across in a very sensitive way. There's nothing flash, brash or hard about her. She's got a natural humility. She got the sympathy vote with her hubby playing away.' He added, 'Ashley Cole comes across as arrogant, whereas Cheryl comes across as friendly, nice and natural and we like that quality in our stars. Simon Cowell clearly spotted that very early on and he's a good judge of character.'

No matter how much she tried to avoid the topic, however, her relationship with Ashley was what many wanted to know about. In an extract, published in *OK!* Magazine, from Girls Aloud's autobiography *Dreams That Glitter*, Cheryl said:

People make mistakes, stuff happens. I believe everyone should be a free spirit. Even in my marriage,

Ashley's a free spirit. I'm not his keeper. I believe in letting people live their lives and be free, so Ashley can have time with his friends when he wants, he can go out when he wants.

I'm not the type of person to ring him and be like: 'Where are you, who are you with, what's happening, what time will you be in, why haven't you answered your phone?' I've been that person in the past and I don't like it.

I won't let anything change me and make me revert to being that type of girl, because it's not me.

Cheryl added that people were 'too judgmental' and, 'I can call my husband all the names, but you can't because you don't know him.' She also said, 'I can't cry any more than I've cried. I can't hurt any more than I've hurt.

'When I said my wedding vows I meant them. I said them for life: for better, for worse. Society has its rules about marriage but I have my own and I'm changing and learning all the time.'

She also said she allowed Ashley to have time with his friends when he wanted. 'I'm not Mrs Perfect, I've made mistakes. I still feel there are things I need to sort out in my head, that some things in my life are a bit up in the air.'

Cheryl also dropped a hint about the future. 'I can't see my future without children. These days there's no reason why you can't have a family and a career. I want a big family and that means I have to make a start soon – so watch this space.'

Cheryl was finally wearing her wedding ring after being without it for so long, when she appeared on Jonathan Ross's chat show on BBC television. She kept fiddling with the £150,000 ring while Ross interviewed her, and it sat next to her £50,000 gold engagement ring, set with a huge square-cut diamond – the first time they had been seen on her left hand for many months.

She told Ross that she deserved her rocky marriage to hit headlines – because she had made money talking about their relationship in the past. 'There's no such thing as a private life in this industry. I spoke openly about my marriage in the past and it's come back to hit me in the face. I learned from the past that you shouldn't do that.'

Such was the impact Cheryl had made by this time that there were even suggestions that Simon Cowell wanted to double her salary for the next series to £1 million.

A studio insider said, 'Cheryl has been an instant hit with viewers and contestants. She initially signed a one-year deal as she wasn't sure how she would fare and Simon didn't want to commit to an unknown quantity. Now he's desperate to get her for a new series and put pen to paper.

'He realises he will have to fight to keep her as Girls Aloud are in talks to do a US tour. So Simon needs to act fast and get her to sign before she has unavoidable commitments. As part of the package there's talk of involving her in another of Simon's shows. Cheryl is flattered.'

The process by which the winner of the contest was chosen meant that Cheryl was mentoring three young hopefuls – Alexandra Burke, 20, Diana Vickers, 17, and

Laura White, 20 – and she opened her heart to them when she took the trio out to dinner.

'Everyone was very relaxed and we opened up about things in our lives and she opened up about things in hers. Cheryl has been through a lot in her life. She told us deep secrets – but we're not telling. She was very open with us. We even had a good old cry,' one of the girls said.

Cheryl-mania was mounting and Girls Aloud fans camped on the streets for chance to meet the girls at their book signing in the West End.

There was no doubting that Cheryl's career had now reached another level. 'I'm not at all the confident person that people think I am. So when I turn up to something like today and there are dozens of people waiting to quiz me it gets a bit daunting. I don't mind answering questions but it's like being at school and being summoned to the headmaster's office.'

She was also determined to stress that, in spite of what many observers had been saying for months by this time, she was not too thin. She adds, 'I'm happy with the way I look, eat properly and exercise. This is probably the healthiest I have ever been. But in the early days all those stories about my weight used to get to me. I would cry about it. But now I don't even read the stuff.'

Bt this point in the series, after a number of recorded episodes, *The X Factor* was going out live and she was afraid of 'messing up'. 'If people expect me to be this shy, quiet girl in the corner they have another thing coming.'

She certainly wasn't being quiet during an interview

with *Attitude* magazine. Cheryl had never been afraid of putting her views clearly and succinctly, and this time it was the Spice Girls who were her target. Throughout their career Girls Aloud had been compared to the groundbreaking fivesome, but Cheryl said she found it infuriating when pop hopefuls told her their ambition was to be 'the new Spice Girls'.

'I think, "Piss off!" We've been around for six years – they were around for 18 months! We recognise what the Spice Girls did, but it really annoys me when you meet girls who go: "We wannabe the next Spice Girls." Yes, they had worldwide domination, but they fell out, bitched about each other and went their separate ways. We've been around all this time, fighting to climb each step of the ladder, putting our hearts into everything.'

At the time of the interview, in October 2008, Girls Aloud were set to hit Number 1 with new single, 'The Promise', having been watched by 11 million viewers performing the number on *The X Factor*.

They'd had 18 Top Ten singles – including three Number 1s – and held the record for the most consecutive Top Ten entries by a UK female group as well as having five platinum albums in their six years together.

Cheryl, who by now was in training for a Red Nose Day Comic Relief climb up Mount Kilimanjaro, was with the girls when they attended the Music Industry Trust Awards at London's Grosvenor House Hotel. It was illustrative of her fame at this stage that a chance remark she made in conversation was soon spread around the world. It concerned her pet Chihuahua, Buster, who had already caught the public eye by peeing on the carpet at one *X Factor* audition and Cheryl mentioned that she would wake in the middle of the night to find her expensive underwear had been buried in the back garden at her home.

'My dog digs holes and puts my knickers in the ground – but then I shouldn't be telling you that. It's disgusting, I have no idea why he would do that.'

That brief aside from Cheryl was flashed around the world once it appeared in print in the UK. Newspapers and radio in Australia, Canada and Hong Kong mentioned it, such now was her fame.

In the comparatively brief time that she had been on *The X Factor*, one of the aspects of the show continually under the microscope was the chemistry among the judges: the boss Cowell, the music old hand Walsh and the two women with that much-discussed 11-year age gap.

Eventually Dannii Minogue shed light on the matter and, as many thought, revealed frictions between the judges – and that her close link with Cowell had faded with Cheryl's arrival. 'This year has been very emotional and I admit I've struggled to deal with it all, especially with Simon,' said Minogue. 'I guess Simon and I don't talk much any more, definitely nothing like last year when I was next to him on the panel and was also the new girl. He moved me away from him and now sits next to Cheryl and is in her ear all the time. It is a snub, but I'm fine. It's nothing compared to what I had to go through last year.' Then, it had been Sharon Osbourne with whom she had been at loggerheads; now it was the sniping from outside the programme that her looks could not compare with Cheryl's.

'Lots of people do taunt me, but I put it to one side and carry on with my job, which I take very seriously. I back my contestants 150 per cent and so much that has been written about me is unfair. I actually talk to Cheryl now more than I talk to Simon. It's a very different atmosphere behind the scenes but I'm strong enough to keep on going and try to ignore all the negativity.'

By the time of Dannii's comments in the *News of the World*, the show's viewing figures had leapt on average by 2 million a week since the arrival of Cheryl, and it was beating its long-term adversary, BBC1's *Strictly Come Dancing*, week after week.

Dannii had to miss some of the auditions because she was filming in Australia, leaving the way clear for Simon and Cheryl to bond, which in turn led Louis Walsh, who used to torment Dannii, to turn to her for support.

'Louis has started to cling on to me now Sharon has gone, which has been a bit odd. I don't know what that's about. I'm fed up about the rumours and whispers. I have already spoken to Simon about next year and he's made it absolutely clear I'll be back. I want to come back, so I will be there.

'I think this is the best judging team the show's had, by a long way. We are all very competitive with each other but that's a good thing. It means the competition is tough and we take our jobs seriously.'

Given the immense interest in every aspect of Cheryl's life generated by *The X Factor* by this time, there was the inevitable risk that a skeleton of one sort or another would emerge from the cupboard. In this case the skeleton in question was her brother Andrew. He had, as we have already heard, a history of convictions and was not able to attend Cheryl and Ashley's wedding in the summer of 2006, as he was behind bars at the time.

Now he went public with private information about Cheryl. It must be said that none of his remarks to a tabloid newspaper were detrimental to her – quite the opposite – yet the very fact that one of her close relatives had decided to talk openly cannot have rested easily with the her.

His message was clear: 'Cheryl wants to help me – but I'm too far gone. I know I'm breaking her heart, but I'm not strong enough to sort myself out.' Andrew was out of jail at the time he spoke, but he had spent a total of nine years in prison by this stage, and he was only 28. 'It tears me up to think I'm causing my little sister so much pain. I've told Cheryl she should be ashamed of me, but she says she loves me and she'll never give up on me.'

She had visited him alone in prison the previous Christmas at Acklington jail in Northumberland, where he was serving four years for violent robbery. At that time she was aware of Ashley's drunken incident with Aimee Walton but it had not yet become public knowledge. Minus any makeup and with her hair scrapped back under a hoody, she cried at the prison as she asked her brother, who had a long history of drug abuse, to let Ashley and her pay for his rehab. But he said, 'Everyone in the visiting hall knew who she was, but she didn't care that other inmates and officers were staring at her and could see her crying. She told me she was my sister and that would never change. She left crying and I was taken back to my cell.

'I've never been any good at talking face to face, but I want her and the rest of my family to know that I'm grateful for all their support and for standing by me when they should have dropped me like a stone. I watch Cheryl on television and think, "Your life is so different to the one you left behind." She tells me I should be inspired by what she's done and that I can turn my back on booze and violence. Instead, like a fool, I go back to the drink and the glue,' he told the *Sunday Mirror*.

The last time he saw his famous little sister had been in September, the day after the birth of their sister Gillian's new baby, Keric when Cheryl drove from London to see her. 'She told me she loved me and I told her I was proud of her on *X Factor*.'

Andrew recalled how Cheryl used to entertain at family parties by putting on little dance shows, and their mother and father scrimped and saved to pay for Saturday-morning dance classes. Their mother put her in beauty contests and talent shows, most of which she won. 'I just idolised her.'

When he was 13, Andrew fell in with the wrong crowd and began drinking lager and cider while Cheryl won a place at the Royal Ballet School. Cheryl tried to tell him that he was an idiot to hang around with the group he was socialising with.

'When I got locked up at 15, she cried her heart out. I've never forgotten how cut up she was. I was the big brother who always looked out for her and suddenly I wasn't there any more.'

Cheryl was only 11 at the time he was first incarcerated and she would visit him with the rest of the family, often they would all be in tears. After his release Andrew eventually breached his parole by getting drunk and fighting outside a pub, and returned to prison for 18 months. When he was free again Cheryl was on the brink of fame with Girls Aloud.

While he served his four-year sentence for attacking and robbing a stranger in Newcastle city centre, Cheryl stayed in touch with letters, phone calls and visits. Although he missed the wedding, Andrew, who had never met Ashley, stuck photographs of the occasion up on his cell wall.

As Andrew was recounting this grim existence and battle with drugs, nothing could illustrate the different paths that the sister and her big brother had taken in life more than the fact that, *Vogue* had approached Cheryl for a cover photoshoot. The girl from Newcastle had made it big time.

The previous month she had been on the catwalk at Naomi Campbell's charity show in a red Jean-Paul Gaultier gown, and had become a fashion icon in that instant. Her wardrobe was filled with designer pieces from Herve Leger and Roland Mouret, and, now confident in her own style,

Cheryl had been choosing most of her outfits for the live *X Factor* shows.

On her feet she would wear stilettos by Christian Louboutin and boots from Dolce and Gabbana; and, with the help of stylist Lisa Laudat, she used high-quality extensions and backcombing on her hair to recreate the sixties starlet look. To complete the transformation, Cheryl dumped harsh lipsticks for subtler pink shades and used Mac Face and Body Foundation on her skin.

It must have been working. An hour-long Channel Five documentary about her was screened and she was constantly being named at the top of polls and lists in many categories from 'best bust' to 'best celebrity hairstyle.' In a Mecca Bingo Top 10 of positive role models for British women, which she won, *Harry Potter* author J. K. Rowling came second, the Queen third. Interestingly, a year earlier Cheryl had been bottom of the same list, an 'honour' now bestowed on Amy Winehouse. *The Times*'s fashion editor declared, 'Clearly the entire country is in love with Cheryl Cole.' The *Daily Star* said she was 'only slightly less popular than God'. The *Sunday Times* said she was 'the Sink Estate Superstar'. And the editor of the women's magazine *Grazia* noted, 'In these times of doom and gloom, all we want is a hug from Cheryl. She is like comfort food for the soul. Everything she says on *The X Factor* is absolutely in tune with the mood of the nation. The time for bitchy TV is over. We want warmth.'

As the series drew towards its conclusion, with Cheryl-mentored Alexandra Burke (the eventual winner) as favourite, there was unanimous praise for Cheryl and the impact she had made.

Louis Walsh was in no doubt about the qualities of his co-judge: 'She's been fantastic on the show, a great addition to the team. She's warm, she is talented and successful. She really connected with Simon, especially over dogs. She brings in her dog and Simon loves it. They love the same things, have a lot in common and have a great sense of humour, so they really get on. Before the live shows she is really, really nervous. Sometimes she stands there shaking. But once she is on screen she is fantastic. Throughout the show she has really cared for her acts. But I am glad she has only one act in the final as I want to beat her.'

Even the normally acerbic Jan Moir in the *Daily Mail* had been won over, writing about when Cowell gave her a hug:

She has, as he would say himself, the potential to be world-class. Yet it was unpleasant to watch. A gesture that somehow managed to be threatening yet oily and proprietorial at the same time – imagine a grizzly cradling a prize salmon, and you get the idea.

Yet no wonder Cowell wants to stick close. It is not just the fact that her act won, but Cheryl Cole is the undoubted star of *The X Factor* this year. Everyone adores her. And alongside the self-satisfied glibness of some of her fellow judges, her homespun and heartfelt Geordie imprecations had a charm all of their own.

'Alexandra, Aye luff ye. Aye yabso lootly luffya

tepeeces. Aye yabso luetly adorr ye,' she said on Saturday, before turning her attention to the audience at home. 'Ah hope yer bums are glued to yer seats,' she cried.

What a cheek. And what a journey we have all been on together. No wonder we will all be back next year for more.

Alexandra Burke duly won the competition and, to no one's surprise, there were tears all round. The stunning 20-year-old, who performed a duet with Beyoncé on the show, simply said, 'Thank you to everyone … I am the happiest girl alive.'

And Cheryl's reaction? 'Just thank you for being you, babe. I absolutely adore you.'

Perhaps Simon Cowell summed it up best: 'I had to really, really twist Cheryl's arm because she didn't know how big she was going to be. I kept saying to her, "If you do this, not only is it going to be great for the show, it's going to be great for you." And she has become the most popular person on TV. More popular than me now. Annoying, but it happens.'

10

GOING UP IN
THE WORLD

A staggering 14.6 million viewers watched the *X Factor* final, the highest-rated entertainment show since the *Only Fools and Horses* Christmas special five years earlier. It was the show that had brought the feel-good factor back to the previously much-criticised Saturday-night television and, although it had been a high-ranking fixture in the schedules prior to Cheryl's arrival, there was doubt in no-one's mind that she had given it, and her own career, a massive boost.

There were, however, misgivings over her role in the programme. A number of fans were worried after seeing her sob uncontrollably after watching her protégé Alexandra Burke clinch the talent show's crown in December 2008. Of concern, too, was the fact that her ribs could clearly be seen through the gaps in her revealing dress.

There was little doubt that she had been under pressure

for the 10 weeks that the show had been aired. Strangely, on the day of the final, she appeared to be more agitated than Alexandra Burke herself.

After Burke was declared the winner, it seemed that *she* was taking care of *Cheryl*, rather than the other way round. The Saturday climax saw Cheryl repeatedly burst into tears – both during the show and again afterwards as she hugged the 20-year-old in her moment of triumph.

Some fans posted their views on showbiz websites and Internet forums. One, calling herself Azalea, said, 'Cheryl looks emaciated!' Another concerned fan, Katie, wrote, 'Cheryl Cole is far too thin.' A poster called Joules said, 'Cheryl looked so thin. Her dress was beautiful, but I think she needs to put on a little weight.' And fan Alexa told of her worries, saying, 'I'm not jealous of Cheryl's figure. In my eyes she is just thin.'

Cheryl wore a metallic-silver dress by British designer Julien Macdonald, which had not only cutouts at the waist but also a plunging neckline. And, as she turned up to hug winner Alexandra, her ribs were clearly on show.

A fan called Shiri said, 'I do not agree that Cheryl Cole looked great on Saturday night – it's hero worship gone too far. She looked emaciated like she was about to snap at any minute. I really, really like Cheryl, but she needs to put on some weight. The cut-out sides further highlighted this fact.'

Cheryl was supported at the final by her Girls Aloud bandmates Kimberley, Sarah and Nicola at the television studios in Wembley, while fellow band member Nadine was in Los Angeles. Ashley was not there, however, as he was preparing to play for Chelsea in Sunday's Premier League game against West Ham.

Cheryl made fun of his absence by posting a jokey sign on her dressing room door, which read, 'Am away training with Chelsea!' An insider said, 'Ashley couldn't be there, but she wanted to make some reference to her husband, which was sweet. She was very happy to have her band there to support her – the girls have been there with her all the way.'

Even agony aunt Dr Miriam Stoppard said, 'I get lots of letters from teens who long to look like their favourite celebrities. They're searching for an identity and often model themselves on TV and pop stars. So Cheryl Cole's appearance on Saturday's *X Factor* final, where her ribs were clearly visible, must have worried parents of teenage girl fans. It's easy to see why she is so popular: Newcastle-born Cheryl has had 20 Top Ten hit singles in Girls Aloud, she's negotiated multimillion-pound ad deals and is the most popular judge on *X Factor*. She's also pretty, glamorous and married to Chelsea and England footballer Ashley Cole. But, even though Cheryl has lost weight, mums and dads don't need to panic – teens may idolise super-slim celebs but that doesn't mean they'll automatically go on a crash diet.'

There was more concern expressed when the *Sun*'s columnist Jane Moore observed:

Cheryl Cole's eye-catching dress was designed to be risqué but it ended up revealing far more than intended. It exposed the innermost fragility of a woman who, despite having a beautiful face, a successful pop career and the accolade of being *The X Factor*'s victorious judge, is clearly troubled.

A woman still visibly wounded by the highly public infidelity of the glamorous husband who bought in to the fairytale marriage then swiftly threw it all back in her face.

All the hair extensions, panstick make-up and fancy frocks in the world can't hide the dead eyes of a woman betrayed …

As I said at the time of Ashley's betrayal, they don't have children so she should dump him and find someone who deserves her love. Now, more than ever, she should take that advice.

Not surprisingly, Alexandra Burke's interpretation of Cheryl's state of mind and her marriage was somewhat different. 'Cheryl is the most beautiful person I've ever met – outside and inside. She has become my friend for life.'

The new star also revealed she had been invited to the Coles' house in Surrey for Sunday lunch, to exchange presents and to meet the couple's families. And she insisted that Ashley and Cheryl were still in love with each other: 'I've met Ashley twice and he is a lovely guy. I can say for sure that they are madly in love. You can just tell. Ashley has been really supportive to me. The first time I sang "Listen", Cheryl rang me up the next day and said she couldn't stop watching the performance.

'They were watching the repeat on the Sunday together. Ashley came on the phone shouting, "You killed it! Absolutely wicked song!"

'She gave me an angel-wing necklace, which I have been wearing ever since. I've got her a friendship bow. It is a piece of antique jewellery which has been cleaned up and set. And I've got a print of us on stage after being told I'd won. I'm in complete shock.'

Alexandra confirmed that Cheryl had banned her from having any boyfriends so that she could concentrate on developing her career. 'Cheryl has been telling me to stay away from boys. She said, "Take this chance with both hands while you've got it. Don't have one hand being led astray."'

As the momentous year for Cheryl drew to a close, she was at the top of every popularity poll that came out, high up on every Review of the Year. She was Superdrug's Beauty Icon of the Year as well as *Heat* magazine's Fittest British Female Celebrity Body.

Young fans on social networking site Bebo said she was their top girl of 2008, beating teenage actress Emma Watson, who plays Hermione Granger in the *Harry Potter* movies, into second place. *Tatler* said she was the Best-Dressed Person of the Year and *OK!* magazine had a readers' poll with several categories, and Cheryl seemed to win virtually all of them.

She was their Star of the Year with three times as many votes as the runner-up, Jordan. She was also WAG of the Year, with more than twice as many votes as Victoria Beckham, and Most Stylish Star, again ahead of Victoria.

She didn't win Most Shocking Celebrity News: that marked the early death in New York of the *Brokeback Mountain* and Oscar-winning *Dark Knight* star Heath Ledger, but her marriage trials with Ashley did come in second behind the 28-year-old actor's early demise.

Ashley wasn't quite as popular, topping a Britain's Most Reviled Celebrity list ahead of foul-mouthed chef Gordon Ramsey and former Atomic Kitten Kerry Katona.

The invitation that had been extended to Cheryl the previous year, to appear in *Vogue*, was accepted, and she duly adorned the cover of the February issue; it was one of the most prestigious magazine covers in the world. She also gave an interview to the magazine, in which she touched on the two topics that everyone wanted to discuss with her: Ashley and her weight.

The time during which his behaviour and their marriage came under public scrutiny was 'horrendous', she said, adding, 'Well, you only have to read the girl's story. Can you imagine? Saying all that stuff about a married man in that state? I mean, to be honest, I feel sorry for her.' She added, 'But look, Ashley's young and he's got a young mentality – for his age anyway.'

She continued, 'He's learning. He has a beautiful soul, he's a really nice guy and I'm not stupid, you know. I'm really not. I know what I'm doing. I've had enough knocks in the past to know what the circumstances are, and I'm happy. If other people aren't, then that's their problem.'

And as for her weight, she told *Vogue* that in 2003, during her first year as a Girls Aloud member, she burst into tears when she could not fit into a pair of jeans and embarked on the Atkins Diet. 'I actually went up to a size 29 [waist],' she said.

'I remember being in Selfridges and taking these size 28s into the changing room and not being able to get them on, and then getting on the scales and crying because I was nine and a half stone. Nine and a half stone when I'm only 5ft 3in. Jennifer Aniston was doing something called the Atkins Diet at the time and I thought I'd give it a try.

'The record company had just moved us into this hotel called K West and I remember I ate the same thing from room service – chicken in cream sauce with a couple of carrots – every night, for weeks, and I just felt horrible. But I was on this mission.'

Cheryl told the magazine she was a worrier and revealed she once suffered from clinical depression: 'That's one of my problems – I do worry about things. I'm probably going to end up dying with worry. I was clinically depressed once after a bad relationship. We have it in the family.'

Cheryl even discussed the infamous incident with the cloakroom attendant: 'I never denied hitting her and I would have hit her again at the time. That's what we were taught on the estate – you have to defend yourself and that's what I was doing.'

She told another interviewer of the position she was in the previous year, saying, 'I had got into such a deep hole of badness – a lot of negative stuff. Until X Factor there was this thing that I was the gobby bitch of the band. Yes,

I'm opinionated, but I wasn't this person I was reading about. I just thought I'd sit on the panel and have a laugh at the nut jobs. Then it escalated.'

There was another award for Cheryl, in addition to those unofficial ones from newspapers and magazines, when she and the other girls won the Best Single category at the Brit Awards. She said that it seemed 'a bit surreal' but added that the award should scotch any notion that the band was on the verge of splitting up. 'We have just won a Brit, voted for by the public and us being here shuts that question up,' she said.

Unlike the previous year, Ashley was with her this time and could be seen smiling and clapping as his wife accepted the award on stage. Although it was a glittering occasion and a night on the town in the manner that had become synonymous with Girls Aloud, there was a far more gruelling event ahead, at least for two of the girls.

Cheryl and Kimberley Walsh were to take part in the arduous eight-day trek in Tanzania, culminating in climbing Mount Kilimanjaro to raise money for Comic Relief, which was to be filmed and aired in the run-up to Red Nose Day on 13 March. Cheryl – dressed in the team uniform of tracksuit bottoms and Red Nose Day T-shirt – added that, while she and Kimberley Walsh may not look glamorous, they would act as a crutch for each other.

'If we didn't have each other I think I'd struggle to get up there,' she said, 'so I think we're at a bit of an advantage having each other.'

Kimberley agreed: 'The makeup and hair thing's

obviously not good. The comfort's good, the clothes are comfy and that's more important.'

The pair were to attempt to reach the top of Africa's highest mountain along with Gary Barlow, Alesha Dixon, Ben Shephard, Radio 1 presenter Chris Moyles, Denise van Outen, Fearne Cotton and Ronan Keating.

The challenge was to 'raise a mountain of cash' to provide people in Tanzania with mosquito nets that could protect against fatal malaria. It had not been an easy training regime so far as the celebrities tried to prepare for Kilimanjaro's crippling altitudes, and some of the team had been working harder than others.

Moyles said, 'I've been running, walking, not drinking – that's the hardest. The last couple of weeks me and a couple of the boys have been training in an oxygen chamber, which is ridiculously stupid.'

He added that he was looking forward to his first drink and hoped it would be at the top of the mountain: 'At the Mount Kilimanjaro Arms, apparently it's lovely, so I can't wait to get there,' he said.

The nine celebrities were to start their climb up Mount Kilimanjaro, which stands 19,340 feet above sea level, at the end of February. Already the training was taking its toll. 'The blisters are horrendous on me,' Cheryl revealed. 'We're not going up there, though, for the good of our health. We're going to try to save lives through the charity, so we've got a different incentive.'

She even joked how she and Kimberley hoped Gary would serenade the group at some point with some Take

That tunes: 'We wanted to take like some sort of little banjo so we could have "Back for Good" around the campfire; that'd be lovely,' she laughed.

'I actually put myself forward for this so the rest of the girls were all, like, "What were you thinking?" ... but they're all really supportive and will be going to rednoseday.com and supporting us and watching the climb and raising money for us, which is amazing.'

Cheryl was 'bulking up' for the climb and was also walking 12 miles a day on a treadmill as part of her get-fit regime. She was training so hard that at one stage she badly bruised her toe. She also became the 'speaking clock' for a day when callers to the line were told the time by her in her Geordie brogue. It was all part of Comic Relief, and 10 pence from every one of the 69,000 calls made during the day she was supplying the voice went to the charity.

It was illustrative of the life that Cheryl was leading by this stage that no sooner had she helped launch the Kilimanjaro climb than she took an 11-hour flight to Los Angeles, where she was linking up with hip-hop star Will.i.am, the Black Eyed Peas rapper who had asked her to work on new songs with him.

It was a great move for Cheryl, as Will.i.am – real name William James Adams, Jr – was one of the biggest stars after work he had done for President Barack Obama.

By the end of February Cheryl and the other celebrities were flying to Africa in a plane with a specially painted red nose, and their climb was due to start at 6am on 1 March. Boyzone frontman Ronan Keating nearly missed the outbound flight after his connection from Dublin was delayed by an hour and a half, and he had to be driven across the Heathrow tarmac in order to catch the waiting flight.

The group had a briefing from Jeremy Gane, a tour operator who was leading the climb, and they also had briefings from two doctors who would be going with them.

They were all getting an early night before setting off at dawn the next day on their trek through the rainforest, where it would be very hot and humid and it was expected that it would take them three days to reach their base camp.

Day One saw the group trek for four hours through the rainforest, and Ronan Keating filmed a video-diary entry from the camp. 'We're finally here, we've reached first camp. Today wasn't too tough a day. We took about four and a half hours to climb different terrain than what I imagined. We were in forest for most of the day but it was amazing. Everybody, all the team and all the crew, did really well, so a great success.'

Cheryl and the others had already raised more than £500,000. Keating added, 'This is our home for the next week and a bit. It's small enough but to be honest I think it's plenty of room. They're one-man tents so there's only one of us in each tent. I've got my gear, it's all here, we've got a little mattress. It's quite cosy and cool. I don't mind sleeping in a tent: I go camping with the kids once or twice a year and you kind of get used to it and it's a nice atmosphere.'

Fellow Girls Aloud member Kimberley said it was 'scary' and 'really daunting' but that there was 'no turning back'. She added, 'There's been a lot of anticipation, about four months' worth I'd say. Not too many things really faze me in life but this really has done. I just think it's so far removed from anything I've ever done or probably will ever do again that it's really kind of been hard for me to get my head around.

'I've been struggling to sleep and all sorts of things and it's just that subconscious knowing that you're going to do something that you really have no idea what it's going to be like.

'There's been a lot of anticipation, so to a point I'm just glad to be here, so actually, whatever happens in the next eight or nine days, I'm doing it now, so there's no turning back at this point.' But she added, 'It feels good to be here and be in such a different environment.'

Cheryl and the rest walked for seven hours the following day, and many of them had to use two hand-poles to help them cope with the rocky terrain.

Gary Barlow, who was suffering from a bad back, described what they were going through: 'The girls tend to lead and us boys follow up behind – I slow them down because my back is probably a three out of ten.

'But everyone is brilliant – especially the guides – and all the girls keep offering to take my day pack from me, bless them. We were all making each other laugh as we walked by replicating the sounds we make on the BT Speaking Clock and adding new ones – both artificial and natural (we had beans last night). The scenery is spectacular – we walked across one of the biggest ridges, the remnants of an old volcano crater. We are at about 11,500 feet now and you can really tell that the air is getting thinner and the temperature is colder.'

The celebrities almost suffered their first serious injury when Alesha Dixon took a tumble while urgently answering the call of nature. She disappeared behind some bushes where she slipped and rolled several yards down a steep ledge. But the group knew she had survived when her distinctive laughter rang out.

Alesha might have been the first to suffer, but there were to be more casualties. Cheryl and Kimberley were hit by altitude sickness and as a result were being monitored by the medical team as they and Denise van Outen complained of severe headaches and nausea after the group made it to 3,500 metres (11,500 feet). The illness brought on by the height they had reached was one of the biggest problems the celebrity climbers faced, understandably so, as in addition to making victims feel unwell, it could possibly be fatal.

The girls were also shaken when a climber from another group was stretchered down the 5,900 metres (19,360 feet) mountain after being knocked out by the sickness.

Cheryl said, 'He looked scared, really frightened. It really shook me up, shook all of us up.' Kimberley added, 'This is hard, the walking is tough, but the altitude makes you feel so different.'

It certainly did, and, by Day Four, Gary Barlow noted in his diary,

Bad night in the camp. Disaster struck in tent six. At midnight we were woken by Fearne calling out for help. She had got up to go to the loo and collapsed on the floor outside from exhaustion and was too weak to move.

Fearne was given an anti-sickness injection but when we woke this morning she still didn't look good. The medics had to give her a full examination before deciding that she could continue.

So, after a good breakfast, all nine of us once again started out on our seven-hour ascent up the rocky terrain which looked like something from Mars. We are now at the coldest camp so far at Lava Tower – 15,000ft. It's colder than anyone could have imagined. The daunting view of the summit sits over us, showing what we still have ahead.

Cheryl said, 'The fun is over. This is unquestionably the hardest thing I have ever done.'

The fun may have been over in Africa, but there were fun and games back in London. While Cheryl and the others were climbing the mountain, Ashley was busy, too, but in a completely different way. He was attracting headlines of his own when he was arrested, handcuffed and taken to a police station after a row at a nightclub. Not what Cheryl would have wanted to hear all those thousands of miles away. That was bad enough, but the details that emerged of his night of shame were to make even more embarrassing reading.

He had initially been arrested on suspicion of being

drunk and disorderly and was held after swearing at police outside the Collection bar in west London. Officers warned him about his behaviour but arrested him at about 2.15am, when he failed to stop swearing or calm down, and he was taken to a nearby police station before being issued an £80 fixed-penalty notice and released about three hours later.

A Scotland Yard spokesman said, 'We can confirm a 28-year-old man was arrested at approximately 2.15am in Brompton Road on suspicion of being drunk and disorderly. He was taken to a central London police station where he was issued with a fixed-penalty notice for being drunk and disorderly and released shortly after 5.30am.'

Bar staff said Ashley had been out drinking with Chelsea captain John Terry and several other Chelsea teammates. General manager Burim Maraj said the popular celebrity hangout closed at midnight but the group stayed inside eating a meal.

The evening had started quite sedately and Ashley had been pictured at a nearby charity event with ex-GMTV presenter Fiona Phillips earlier, when he joined some of Chelsea's first-team squad and more than 300 charity workers, celebrities and supporters for the second annual Chelsea FC and Armani fundraiser.

Children from Chelsea's two official charity partners, CLIC Sargent and Right to Play, joined the players at the Armani Store on Brompton Road where they played against the football team on Scalextric, computer games, table football and pool, according to a statement on the club's website.

Funds were raised for the two charities via an auction that was headed up by Chelsea and England captain John Terry. Other guests included former Formula One supremo Eddie Jordan, ex-Chelsea player Graeme Le Saux, TV presenter Alice Beer and Lady Helen Taylor.

A Chelsea spokesman said when they heard of Ashley's arrest, 'We are aware that Ashley was detained last night. We will want to establish all the facts before commenting.'

Very quickly more details of what had happened began to emerge. Ashley, who racked up a £1,000 bill at the restaurant with teammates, was 'rude' to police after getting frustrated by waiting paparazzi, Burim Maraj was quoted as saying.

The manager said the trio had 'behaved well' before someone apparently took a picture of Ashley, who had dined on a £50 Japanese steak, inside the restaurant. The three players enjoyed a range of drinks, some of which may have been bought for them by other guests, he added.

'People were coming up to them during dinner, men and women. They seemed happy and quite polite – all the players came for a quiet night. I believe there was a photographer inside who took a picture of Cole. He [Ashley] was more frustrated than being drunk, because of paparazzi – it must have been something.

'My staff told me he stopped to speak to police as he left. He was apparently complaining about paparazzi. My staff said he was being rude to the police,' added Maraj, who said that the Chelsea players regularly visited his venue and always behaved well.

The Collection, which opened in 1997, became a favourite on the west London celebrity scene after George Michael threw a birthday party there following his arrest in a Beverly Hills public toilet. Prince Harry and Prince William had visited the club in the past.

Ashley quickly issued a statement: 'I would like to take this opportunity to apologise to the police officers on duty last night for my language. I felt I was being harassed by paparazzi and while complaining to the police about this at the scene they did warn me to calm down, a warning that I regrettably did not heed. I fully appreciate that whatever frustrations I may have had with others that it was completely inappropriate to vent those in conversations with the police. However, I do want to make clear that I swore in frustration at the paparazzi's behaviour. I would never disrespect police officers in any way.

'I take very seriously my responsibilities as a professional footballer. This includes keeping my body in the best condition. Although I had consumed some alcohol earlier in the evening on a night out with friends it had not been excessive. But I accept that the language I used on this occasion was wrong. I regret my actions and how it reflects on myself and Chelsea Football Club.'

Ashley received an £80 police fine for being drunk and disorderly but then Chelsea, by now managed by Dutch disciplinarian Guus Hiddink, fined him £160,000, equivalent to two weeks' wages.

'I talked this morning with Ashley about this situation and he has publicly apologised about his conduct towards the police officer,' Hiddink said. 'We also have internal discipline and it is to be considered internal. Of course I have spoken firmly with him about responsibility and there are rules inside this club regarding going out.

'You have to judge what the circumstances were,' the Dutchman said. 'I tackled him on this behaviour and he was in his opinion harassed a little bit. That is why he reacted like he reacted and he regrets that.'

The *Sun*'s report of the evening contained details of what occurred both inside and outside the restaurant:

A group of champagne-swilling girls invited the stars and some guests they were with into a cordoned-off area. Cole, who earns £92,000 a week, plonked himself on a bar stool. Then as Chelsea skipper Terry and Mancienne mingled, he knocked back a bottle of Japanese Asahi lager.

He clutched a wad of £20 notes as he ordered a round of drinks – and began chatting to a blonde clubber wearing a shiny blue mini-dress and a string of white pearls. The pair touched each other's hands as they got close at the bar. A source at the club said: 'She was stunning and clearly very taken with Cole. They broke off from the main group and were talking quietly alone. There were no free seats at the bar so she stood directly in front of him. She placed her hands on his lap as she leaned in to speak to him, directly into his right ear. At one stage Cole was gesturing with his left hand and she could clearly see his large diamond wedding ring. He was laughing and joking with her."

The report continued by saying, 'But just after midnight Cole's mood turned ugly after he realised a *Sun* photographer had snapped him and the girl. Minders protecting the player took our snapper's camera away.'

Ashley left the club about 30 minutes later, the report continued, heading for a chauffer-driven car. 'But he went into meltdown as more photos were taken. Swearing furiously, he screamed at our photographer to delete the pictures. Cops told him to tone down his aggression. But he continued to rant, telling them to intervene and accusing them of not doing their job.'

After the arrest had become public knowledge, Ashley's legal advisers said that photographing him inside the nightspot breached his privacy under the Human Rights Act and he threatened to sue the *Sun* for aggravated damages if the newspaper published pictures showing him beside a beautiful blonde in the club, the paper said.

A source was quoted as saying, 'Ashley feels his privacy has been invaded by being photographed in the nightclub. He is a great believer in his right to privacy and will take legal action if anyone publishes those photos.'

A friend of the player insisted he and the woman had been engaged in 'an intellectual conversation' – a remark that would subsequently appear in several publications.

The paper went on to describe the photographs in great detail and said Ashley 'looks up at the blonde as she turns her head to the side. Another shot shows Cole deep in conversation with the girl, who smiles and appears enraptured by the discussion.'

The red-top tabloid, the largest-selling daily newspaper in the country, couldn't resist having some fun at his expense by asking, 'What were they discussing?' and coming up with a variety of answers, including the merits of quantitative-easing economic policy, how President Obama could promote relations between the US and Iran and whether North Korea's weapons arsenal was a genuine threat.

Friends of Ashley's said he had never met the woman before and he had instructed his representatives to track her down and prove he did nothing wrong and that their conversation was entirely innocent.

Meanwhile, back on Kilimanjaro, plucky Cheryl, still suffering from altitude sickness, had braved a storm high up the mountain and reached the summit in Africa, saying, 'It's been really hard physically and mentally, but I haven't once thought of giving up.'

The contrast between the two Coles could not have been greater: one had battled sickness and the elements for charity; the other, regardless of the rights and wrongs of the case, had ended up being handcuffed and fined. Not only had Ashley left himself wide open for criticism, but the media were about to have a field day with his massive own goal.

Former Liverpool star and now a television soccer pundit Mark Lawrenson was one of the first to put the boot in.

'While his wife Cheryl Cole is climbing Kilimanjaro for charity, the Chelsea left-back is out on a Wednesday night getting arrested. It doesn't get much worse than that.

'I don't think going out on a Wednesday night before a game on a Saturday is that bad or unforgivable. Most clubs have a 48-hour curfew before a game. Furthermore, from what I hear, Cole is not a big drinker, he's a good trainer and is also a highly tuned athlete, so would not find it hard to recover comfortably in time for Chelsea's next game. Where I think he deserves to be fined two weeks' wages is because he's supposed to be a role model.

'That is something that Chelsea have to do, regardless of whether Guus Hiddink is manager for five months or five years. You have to set standards ... Unfortunately, it's another hammer blow for Cole. He is now painted as the archetypical spoilt footballer: talented, gifted, rich, showbiz wife, trappings of fame and fortune ... But what Cole has forgotten is that he's a marked man. He needs to remember he's in the spotlight for wrong reasons, so he needs to be on his best behaviour at all times.

'I think he regrets ever doing that book for a start – and particularly complaining about getting £55,000 a week. But what comes through out of this is that I'm not even sure whether Cole is bothered about his public image anymore. He has been in good form this season. He's enjoyed something of a renaissance. So he can probably just turn around and say, "I don't care what people think any more." His actions this week suggest that he is indeed past caring.'

However, criticism from 'Lawro' was nothing compared with the vitriol that dripped from the pens of the women who were commentating on Ashley's behaviour.

Television's Lorraine Kelly asked, 'Just what exactly is wrong with Ashley Cole?' She continued,

Why does he persist in behaving as though he is a single bloke when he is married to one of the most beautiful, desirable and popular women in Britain?

As wife Cheryl struggles to the top of Mount Kilimanjaro combating aches and pains, blisters and bruises, chronic fatigue and altitude sickness, her buffoon of a husband is out on the town boozing and chatting to star-struck young blondes ...

The Chelsea star has already badly let down Cheryl after playing away from home in December 2007 and his antics caused her great pain. Cheryl's weight plummeted and she was in turmoil. After a lot of soul searching, she forgave her cheating husband and decided to wipe the slate clean and start again ...

Cole has let himself and his team down, but most of all he has humiliated and embarrassed his long-suffering wife.

Fiona McIntosh, writing in the *Sunday Mirror*, said,

As if Cheryl Cole didn't have enough on her plate. Mud, rain, crippling altitude sickness and not a Carmen roller in sight, her trek up Kilimanjaro for

Comic Relief has turned into a wholly unglamorous nightmare.

Now her plonker of a husband has gone and got himself arrested outside a nightclub back in London. Whatever pain Cheryl is in now, it's nothing to the pain Ashley will be in when she gets home. And quite right, too ...

How many more chances can she give him until he gets the message that a good marriage is based on mutual support and respect?

Carol Malone in the *News of the World* wasn't in the mood to take prisoners either:

What kind of idiot is this man? Is he in possession of even a single brain cell? Doesn't he understand that Cheryl – currently on a charity climb up Kilimanjaro – can go on forgiving him for only so long before she starts looking stupid and gullible? How long can this girl, who has worked like a demon to earn her success and is currently at the top of her game, continue being married to a man who not only hurts and humiliates her but also continuously drags her into the mire where he resides sullying her hard-earned reputation? ...Can't he go to a restaurant without chatting up women? Can't he behave like a decent human being when his wife's away raising money for disadvantaged people who don't have what he has? ...

The time's coming when Cole's reputation will

impact not just on his wife's sanity but on her career, her reputation and her attractiveness to people who might want to employ her. She will become tainted simply by her association with him. And that really *will* be the end.

The *Daily Mail*'s Alison Pearson joined the ever-increasing club who had Ashley in their sights.

Poor Cheryl Cole. Despite risking her mascara to scale the heights of Mt Kilimanjaro and helping to raise half a million pounds for Comic Relief in the process, it was her useless husband Ashley Cole who made the headlines ... Let's hope that the Kilimanjaro experience has given Cheryl the strength to do what needs to be done. Meanwhile, Ashley might like to make a Comic Relief donation that matches the sum raised by his plucky wife. A week's pay – 80 grand – would be a start. If not, Ashley could do a climb of his own, preferably up an active volcano.

The *Daily Star* was even more direct, awarding him its Plonker of the Week prize, saying: 'Cole has proved many times he is the classic case of someone who believes he is more important than he is. Cheryl Cole has become a national treasure, while the Chelsea and England left-back still appears an arrogant, big-headed, yobbish fool.'

There was widespread speculation that Cheryl would give Ashley a tongue lashing when they were reunited, but she was keeping tight-lipped about her plans when she and the rest of the celebrities returned to the UK. They were happy to answer questions about their climb, but queries about her reaction to her husband's night on the tiles were most definitely banned.

What would happen next in their marriage? It couldn't get any worse than this.

Could it?

11

THE YEAR OF CHERYL

There was no doubt about it – 2009 was to become the Year of Cheryl. Her first season on *The X-Factor* had given her career an astonishing boost and elevated her to stardom and that success was to continue its upward path in the next 12 months.

Hardly a day went by without her being mentioned in the press. Her every move, action or comment was reported and invariably analysed, her appearance, her fashion sense, her style and even her politics were given microscopic attention. Any remark she made in the interviews that she gave was instantly picked up on by all those hungry for her thoughts. And nowhere did this apply more than to her marriage with Ashley.

Cheryl's figure was a source of constant attention: was she too thin, was she regaining weight, weight that she may not even have lost in the first place? Surely she was as near perfect as she could be. Apparently not. Who said so? Cheryl herself.

In comments to *Grazia* magazine she said it 'destroyed' her when girls got hung up about their bodies: 'I don't want to be thin, I hate looking thin. I don't want to be up and down like a lollipop lady. It's not a good look … I hate that women feel guilty about eating – just treat yourself.'

Yes, she did lose weight, but that was when she was touring with the band.

'I challenge anyone to do the ridiculous amount of dancing and exercise we do day in day out and not lose weight and tone up. But I don't like the thin look. I love curves. I hate the fact I have no bum. I get called flatty batty.

'In an ideal world I'd have smaller boobs. I'm a 32D, which is ridiculous for my size, and boobs are hard to dress. I hate looking booby. You can look really cheap very quickly. I'd love to have more junk in me trunk. Ideally, a body like Jennifer Lopez. But I'd dress differently to her. I'd dress like I do now. I'm happy with my style and I'm totally in love with fashion because I've learnt by making every mistake in the book.'

This frankness, this openness about herself, which bordered on self-depreciation at times, might have appeared to indicate self-obsession in some, but in Cheryl it was simply an honesty, a trait that was as endearing as it was natural.

She was voted *Glamour* magazine's Best-Dressed Woman of the Year – the previous year it was Kate Moss – to add to the seemingly never-ending list of awards she was receiving, and *FHM* readers said she was 'the sexiest woman in the world'.

In May it was reported that her new deal with *The X-Factor* was to earn her £1.25 million a year, putting her in the Anne Robinson category of female big earners on television. And there was to be a 'golden handcuffs' payment of £1.1 million to host other major shows.

'This is an enormous coup for ITV,' one television insider said. 'Cheryl has major appeal across ages and genders for her beauty and down-to-earth personality. Times are tough in telly land, like everywhere else. But the option of bringing someone of Cheryl's calibre into the station is too good to pass up. They're discussing whether Cheryl should host a chat show. But they also know the void left by Cilla Black in light entertainment has never really been filled. Basically, they want her to become the Queen of ITV.'

An *X Factor* source echoed that sentiment: 'Cheryl is the nation's darling. We may be living in the toughest economic times in decades, but when someone helps a show pull nearly 15 million viewers – as on last year's *X-Factor* final – then you have to pay to keep them on board. Cheryl made last year's series. She gave us glamour and helped bring in the young viewers that we desperately need to woo advertisers. She's worth every penny.'

Although ITV, like the rest of the entertainment industry, had been hit hard by the recession, *The X-Factor* was seen as the channel's flagship show, and its budget had been given a £6 million boost. 'Things have been strained because everybody is under pressure to produce the best show they can for as little cash as possible,' the source added.

'Advertisers are leaving ITV in droves, and it's advertisers who help ITV raise the funds to make their shows. At one point, it seemed auditions could even be stopped. But it's sorted now and we're sure there's going to be another stonking series.'

There was certainly enough time and money spent in ensuring that the series was a hit. Cheryl and Dannii, for example, enjoyed the services of a stylist – paid for by programme makers Talkback – when the show went out live.

Before then, they were reported to pay out of their own pockets for any advice they received, Cheryl relying on Victoria Adcock, who styled her ultra-feminine look for Girls Aloud while Dannii used her assistant, Tori King, and aimed for edgier looks, often using Aussie designers Ralph & Russo and J'Aton.

They used to share a hair and makeup artist, but that arrangement came to an end and Lisa Laudat, who looked after Cheryl on the most recent Girls Aloud tour, did her hair and makeup for all the shows.

It would almost be easy to forget, in view of the success that Cheryl was having, that her marriage to Ashley Cole was one involving *two* successful people. Ashley, after all, was still one of the best left-backs in the world and was held in great esteem in the game. He was also, in spite of the publicity that he inevitably seemed to attract, liked by many of those who knew him.

He helped Chelsea to finish third in the Premiership, reach the semi-final of the Champions League before they lost narrowly to the eventual winners, Barcelona, and he picked up the Man of the Match award when Chelsea beat Everton 2–1 in the FA Cup final. His international career also ensured that every game he played was a high-profile one and he was a key component in the push to get England into the 2010 World Cup finals in South Africa.

None of these seemed to matter to some spectators, however, and he was still regarded as 'Cashley' by many of them. A costly slip in a qualifying match against humble Kazakhstan was his England low point, and it led to the boo boys targeting him at Wembley.

'There are times when you don't like football, just like any job,' he had to admit as the season drew to a close. 'There were times when I didn't enjoy it. I hope it turns now. I don't think I was the worst player against Kazakhstan. But everyone knows it wasn't about football, so there is nothing I can do. I can just try to show people I can play as well as I can to change opinion.

'I feel like I am enjoying my football again and if I play well then I will change people's minds. I just want to win things, just win and hopefully win something with England. If I score the winning goal for England at the World Cup then maybe they will like me again.'

He had had an operation on a long-term injury problem in summer 2007. 'I played with it in the last World Cup and I was rubbish, so I just wanted the injury finished and then I could get back to my best. I did it at Arsenal and I came to Chelsea within six or seven months and didn't want to have the operation straightaway.

'When I first came to Chelsea I couldn't kick the ball and it was pointless me playing really. But I tried to play through the pain for the manager who bought me. Now I feel fit and feel how I did when I was at Arsenal. I've two ankles I can run on, that's the reason I'm playing well. I can run up and down again and I can kick the ball again.

'The operation took the pieces of bone away so I can move easily now. I shouldn't have delayed, but you learn from these things. Now I'm happy with the way things are going. This is the best I've felt.'

Earlier he pointed out, 'I've dealt with the abuse a lot now. It seems like every game I get it. I try to block it out as much as I can and get on with my game. Sometimes it can affect me, sometimes it doesn't. Sometimes it makes me want to prove people wrong. Sometimes you want them to still love you and it's not going to happen, but that's life.

'Arsenal will always have a place in my heart, but I don't see Arsenal fans singing my name in the next few weeks or years. As a person, you do have to respect someone's views, opinions and values that they hold in life. But I don't see them forgetting and I don't blame them. I've got to get on with my life. There's nothing I can do.'

Cheryl was in Birmingham for her 26th birthday at the end of June and Ashley surprised her during her lunch break with flowers, a gift and balloons.

Later in the week they celebrated in style in London. Dannii Minogue was invited and she arrived at the bash in a shimmering off-the-shoulder grey satin cocktail dress and gold peep-toe shoes. Cheryl opted for a see-through Alexander McQueen creation, which gave the impression of being both frontless and backless. The £4,000 frock was teamed with a pair of skin-coloured £495 Christian Louboutin sling-back heels when she went for a meal with Ashley and her mother Joan at the May Fair hotel. Joan wore a figure-hugging minidress that was so tight and smooth that some observers speculated that, as there was no visible panty line, she might even have 'gone commando' for the evening. One partygoer said, 'Cheryl's dress was a real head-turner. It was the talking point on the night.

'Most of the girls weren't sure – but the lads certainly liked it.

'Cheryl is a beautiful girl and by wearing that dress she proved she has her own individual style.'

After their meal the trio then headed to the Vanilla nightclub for the party, also attended by *X-Factor* chief Simon Cowell and Girls Aloud bandmates Kimberley and Nicola. As well as Dannii, her boyfriend Kris Smith and Cheryl's protégés Alexandra Burke and Diana Vickers were there. *Xtra Factor* presenter Holly Willoughby also partied with husband Dan Baldwin. Baby Spice Emma Bunton was there with partner Jade Jones.

Every guest at the star-studded bash was given a piece of birthday cake to take home – in a pink box. The cake had a loving message to Cheryl from Ashley in icing, which read, 'To my little star, happy birthday.'

Ever the romantic, Cheryl turned matchmaker as *The X-*

Factor moved into top gear. She became upset when teenage hopefuls Kirsty Weightman and Jack Stuckey revealed that they called off their wedding plans just two weeks earlier before their appearance on the show.

When Jack admitted it all came to an end because of arguments over washing-up and nights out, Cheryl decided to act. She told them not to split over such a petty row.

When the couple – whose stage name was Combined Effort – belted out Starship's 'Nothing's Gonna Stop Us Now', Jack forgot his words and had to be coaxed by his ex, who held his hand. Clearly moved, Cheryl told him, 'I think she still loves you, you know, Jack.' And Simon Cowell added, 'I think you should ask Kirsty back out.'

Finally, Jack submitted to Cheryl's pleading and the teenagers make up on stage – to the delight of the 2,000-strong Cardiff audience.

The reason that Cheryl's face adorned magazine covers and newspaper front pages wasn't simply that she invariably looked terrific – she sold, too. Her sexy yet refreshing image was a guarantee in the cutthroat world of publishing that sales would increase.

The 'Cheryl Factor' was emphasised by the news that she had landed a £500,000 deal with the beauty label L'Oreal of Paris to front a major TV ad campaign, starting in autumn.

Cheryl would also feature in glossy magazines and on billboards for the company, following other famous beauties including Beyoncé, Linda Evangelista, Jane Fonda and Jennifer Aniston in promoting the brand.

'Cheryl is a beautiful, sassy girl who is just perfect for this particular job. She is everything that young women aspire to. She has amazing skin and hair and had everything L'Oreal was looking for – even though she is a singer and not a professional model.'

It would mean, however, that Cheryl would not be able to dye her hair any more wild shades – such as the plum-colour she had tried out a couple of weeks earlier. A close pal revealed, 'Cheryl dyed her hair for a magazine fashion shoot but went back to her original brunette within a couple of days. Since then she has been busy working on her solo album.'

Cheryl was even making political statements, of a kind. Conservative leader David Cameron had once said she was 'the most fanciable' of Girls Aloud, but when Cheryl was asked by Q magazine what she thought of him, she said, 'David Cameron. Brrrrr. Slippery, isn't he? We've always been Labour in our family, it just feels wrong not to be. Better the devil you know.'

She also admitted what it was like to live with Ashley, saying, 'He hates losing. He talks to me about football, but I don't understand the tactical side of it.' And she revealed that he is 'ridiculously, painfully shy'.

Cheryl was continually featuring in stories over which she had no control or direct involvement. When England football manager Fabio Capello announced he wanted no repeats of the WAG frenzy from Germany at the 2010 World Cup, Cheryl's name was one that the press automatically now linked with WAG-mania – even though, as we have seen, she was comparatively low-key during the 2006 tournament.

'I hope we will be there for a very long period but the players will have one day with their family, with the girls and with their friends,' Capello said. 'It will be one day a week, after each game, and that is enough. That's it. We are there to play football, not for a holiday. If they do not want to come for the day, then they should stay at home.'

Someone who was definitely staying at home, if the gossip columnists were to be believed, was Cheryl's mother. It had already been noted how close Cheryl was to Joan, and they had been seen out and about together on numerous occasions, often as a 'threesome' with Ashley; and it is interesting to note a brief item that appeared in the *Sunday Express* gossip pages on 27 September that year:

It is definitely a case of 'girls allowed' in England defender Ashley Cole's £6million Surrey roost, where his mother-in-law Joan Callaghan has moved in and been given free rein to redecorate the bedrooms and turn one of them into a nursery, in anticipation of her dear daughter Cheryl becoming pregnant.

Joan is desperate for Cheryl to become a mum ...

Newcastle-born Cheryl has promised her mother, and her hubby, that they can start trying for a baby only after she has given birth to another bundle of noise, her new album. Not that she's at home much for Ashley to practise his manoeuvres, busy as she is outflanking her counterpart Alesha Dixon on *Strictly*

Come Dancing, and judging would-be Girls Aloud singers on *The X-Factor*.

Cheryl loves having her mum there. She knows she can leave everything to her. Ashley feels a bit ground down by the united front of his wife and mother-in-law but he's good-humoured about it.

In the autumn, Cheryl did a clutch of interviews to coincide with her solo album *3 Words* and the single 'Fight for This Love'. Taken in isolation, they revealed snippets of her thoughts and her everyday life; pieced together, they gave a fascinating insight into her state of mind and the attitude she had both to her current success and to her roots.

'Of course there are downsides to my life,' she said. 'I'm still a human being, I still have girlie problems. And there are things you can't do any more – just the normal everyday things you once took for granted. I don't go to the supermarket, for instance. I do my shopping online now. Even answering the door you dash down looking scruffy in your dressing gown to collect a parcel and then suddenly you realise the person recognises you and it's like, "Oh my God! I'm standing here looking terrible in my flipping dressing gown." What's weirder is that I don't feel like someone who is famous until people start reacting like that.

'So in my head I'm running around living a normal life and doing everyday things and suddenly I have to realise that I can't just stroll out there in public and do what I want.

'I'm not complaining but it takes you a while to get your head around that.

'From the moment I step outside my front door – even if it's just to go to the supermarket – I'm working. So looking good and not being caught out can be very consuming.'

She revealed she has even done a 'Julia Roberts' and left the house with hairy armpits. And she added, 'Sometimes I can be so busy I'll totally forget to shave my armpits and will suddenly notice and think, "Oops!"'

Her single was being released at roughly the same time as *The X-Factor* returned to TV screens and she had to admit, 'I think I have turned into a workaholic and when I get a couple of days off I'm itching to get back to work. That's the truth of it. I have my BlackBerry, which I'm always on, even when I'm not in work mode. As soon as I get an email it buzzes and it never stops all day.

'I am the worst technical person ever, though. I can't do any of that MySpace, Facebook or Twitter stuff. I'm no good at it. I don't have any accounts with those websites. People are pretending to be me. I don't know who it is.

'It's really cute when it's a fan but when they are pretending to be me just to stir up things or mislead people then it's not fair.'

And on the subject of football, she wasn't embarrassed to say, 'I wouldn't know the technical side of it. Don't ask me about formations and offside because that's beyond me. But, then again, if you ask Ashley about a key change in a song, he wouldn't know what I was going on about.'

He didn't have any input into her album. 'He is tone deaf,' she said.

She insisted that she had stopped reading the many thousands of words that were now being written about her daily. 'I've spent many years crying myself to sleep over the crap people have written. I avoid it all now, as my tears won't stop them writing whatever they want.'

Tellingly, in an interview with the *Sunday Times*, she admitted, 'I've come to the conclusion that I don't trust anybody in life except my mother and my dogs. I'm scared to let people know how much they mean to me, and it's scary that you can love a small hairy thing so much.'

But she said her marriage was 'happy', describing Ashley as a 'simple person'.

'Nothing's under the surface with him. Nothing's a problem, everything's easy and comfortable. He's a genuinely nice person.' These comments from Cheryl about her husband and how he behaved were to be reproduced many times in the months that lay ahead.

She also admitted that she still felt butterflies in her stomach over him. 'But you always hold that 20 per cent back for yourself. I think it's key for your own sanity. You've got to protect yourself.'

Asked about Ashley's alleged infidelity, she told *Elle* magazine, 'I know from a perspective how it looks but it's not like that. And I'm not a stupid girl. I'm not one of those girls who can't see things for what they are. I've been out with idiots in the past.

She said marriages had to be worked at and were not

'rose-petalled paths that you skip down', adding , 'Love is real and the feelings of love are real. But the thought that everything is going to be rosy and there's never going to obstacles that come in your way, that there is never going to be any testing in life, I'd hate that. I want to experience life. I want to experience the bad to know what the good is.'

She has also said she could not wait to have children: 'Even if all this went tomorrow and I just had my family and my kids and my husband and my parents, I'm happy,' she said.

In spite of these interviews and Cheryl's explanation of how she ran her life, some people were still confused about her relationship with Ashley. The website Confused.com even compiled a nationwide poll of the 50 most confusing things in life, and 'Why hasn't Cheryl Cole dumped Ashley?' came in fourth; and her loyalty to Ashley was seen as more confusing than credit-card interest rates, the laws of cricket, insurance policies and why Stonehenge was built.

Confusing or not, Cheryl and Ashley were among the guests, days later, at the party of the year at Wrotham Hall, where they had married three and a half years earlier, for Simon Cowell's 50th-birthday bash.

The £1 million do was the hottest ticket in town and Cowell flew home via private jet the day before the party to oversee last-minute arrangements.

The celebration took months of planning and had been coordinated by retail king Sir Philip Green and his wife Tina, who had made frequent trips from the couple's home in Monte Carlo to oversee the event with London-based party planners Banana Split, the company who had arranged Cheryl and Ashley's wedding.

Guests included some of the most powerful movers and shakers in the music industry including Elton John; actor Kevin Spacey; supermodels Naomi Campbell and Kate Moss and her boyfriend Jamie Hince; Gordon Ramsay and his wife Tana; Andrew Lloyd Webber and his wife Madeleine; Michael Winner; Myleene Klass; and Cowell's ex-girlfriends former singer Sinitta, TV presenter Terri Seymour and ex-glamour model Jackie St Clair.

After the party, it was back to work with 2009's *X Factor*. Simon Cowell's, criticism of Cheryl as a mentor reduced her to tears and some of the talent show viewers also laid into her on websites. The music mogul accused Cheryl of not doing her mentoring job properly and twice made her tearful. He blamed Cheryl for letting down two of her acts with her poor choice of songs for them and said of Lloyd Daniels's rendition of Leona Lewis's 'Bleedin' Love', 'The song was too big for you. I put the blame with the girl on my right, who is not working with you properly, not understanding you properly and not giving you the right material to survive in this competition. You are not being directed properly.'

And he criticised Rikki Loney's version of Aretha Franklin's 'Respect', adding, 'You have gone from a pub singer to a wedding singer and it's down to the song choice.'

Twenty-two-year-old Rikki later said Cheryl was so terrified before her solo routine that her own acts had to calm her down. 'She was really, really nervous. She kept saying, "I can't believe how nervous I am," and we kept reassuring her. She said she couldn't believe that we were telling her it would be OK – like we were being her mentor.

'I should have listened to Whitney Houston [his guest mentor]. They advised me to change. I'd have liked to, but there just wasn't any time. It was literally 24 hours before the performance. I couldn't do it. Too much work had gone on – days had been spent working out the routine.'

Rikki added, 'I knew "Respect" was a massive risk. It didn't pay off.'

He revealed that Cheryl wept after losing the first of her acts. He said, 'Cheryl was really upset. She felt really sad. She felt it was her fault.'

Cheryl put those attacks behind her and triumphantly unveiled her new single 'Fight for This Love' to millions of viewers on the show.

Her performance, in red military-style tunic with a deep-cut front and black trousers slashed at the sides, was stupendous and Cowell and Dannii Minogue gave her a standing ovation.

Cowell said, 'This is going to pain me but that was incredible – really, really incredible. And I will tell you, you can be in my category any day. I know there's been a lot of stick flying around this week about your performance. It's really hard to come out from here up there. That was an incredible routine. A great performance. And unfortunately you will be Number 1 next week.'

A thrilled Cheryl, who had earlier accused Cowell of getting on her nerves, said, 'I really enjoyed that. It felt a bit of a blur. It took me right back to my days of *Popstars: The Rivals*.' Ashley and Cheryl's bandmates Sarah, Kimberley and Nicola were all in the audience to watch her triumph. It encapsulated her appeal. She was sexiness personified, yet endearing with her fun and energy.

Simon Cowell, as usual, was right. 'Fight for This Love' went straight to Number 1. Within a day of being released, it sold more than 134,000 copies and was set to be the fastest-selling single of the year so far.

By now Cheryl and Ashley were *the* couple in the spotlight. Every move was scrutinised in detail and there were practically daily updates on whether Cheryl was wearing a ring or not; sightings of the couple were recorded in almost forensic detail.

Even a planning application, hardly the most showbiz of stories, received massive coverage when they had a proposal for an underground swimming pool at their Godalming home thrown out by planning officials.

The couple wanted to build the 12x5-metre pool and 'a modest gym and spa' beneath their mansion to escape the prying eyes of paparazzi and reporters. When their original application was rejected by Guildford Borough Council on the grounds that it was 'disproportionate' to the size of the house, the pair appealed, only to be told it been dismissed, despite their claims that their celebrity status should have made it an 'exceptional' case.

They had argued through their planning consultant that they had a right to privacy in their home, set in five hectares of land, and, speaking on their behalf, Jonathan Phillips said they could not go to public gyms and swimming pools.

He wrote to the Planning Inspectorate, which considered the appeal, saying, 'It is also not reasonable to suggest that they could utilise external health and fitness facilities because (drawing upon previous experience of using such facilities), they have been subject to disturbance and aggravation from paparazzi and members of the public.'

It was claimed the couple needed to stay fit and healthy because of their jobs, but that press intrusion made it impossible for them to have an outdoor pool. He wrote, 'The press is particularly keen to photograph intimate episodes in the couple's lives and being bedecked in swimsuits exposes the couple to greater likelihood of intrusion, particularly from overflying aircraft equipped with sophisticated photographic equipment.'

The couple cited a planning proposal submitted by guitar superstar Eric Clapton, who was allowed to build a taller fence at his home to stop being harassed, but the planning inspector said the circumstances were different.

Then, in November Cheryl appeared on *The X-Factor* one Saturday without her wedding ring on. The gossip started again even though a source at the show tried to explain it away by saying Cheryl had merely forgotten to put it on after washing her hands. On the next night's results show, however, the ring did not reappear.

A week earlier Cheryl had been having a web chat with a fan and she said, 'I believe in soul mates, yes, but I believe you also have to work at love.' She then added, 'I happen to believe your soul mate doesn't have to be your partner – your soul mate could be your best friend, your sibling, it doesn't have to be the person you marry.'

By the middle of November, Cheryl – who had spent £14,000 on a miniature Hummer car for Ashley to ride around the grounds of their home in, which came complete with £5,000 high-spec extras and designer 'bling' – had earned an estimated £6.9 million through TV and sponsorship deals and her new solo career.

A string of deals, topped by her role as a judge on *The X Factor*, which netted her £1.75 million in two years, meant her total wealth was now about £12 million. With Girls Aloud she had made £1.5 million plus an expected £1 million from her solo music career. Added to that was her L'Oreal deal plus extra money from a new calendar, and a further £400,000 from modelling and interviews.

Experts reckon that was nothing compared with what she could make in the future. One source said, 'There's much more in the pipeline. She has the potential to be massive and leave other WAGs behind.'

A new firm, Cheryl Cole Ltd, had just been set up and there was the possibility of a book deal. She was also said to be planning to launch her own fashion label in the UK and US, with a perfume range expected to follow.

At the end of November 2009 she tried to put any rumours about marital strife to rest as she stepped out with Ashley to celebrate her bandmates' birthdays.

As Cheryl proudly wore her engagement ring, the couple

showed a united front as she partied with Sarah Harding and Kimberley Walsh at Kanaloa in Farringdon in London. She had already felt compelled to post a picture of herself on Twitter wearing the £160,000 sparkler, saying, 'Three words. Diamonds Are Forever.'

In the middle of December her own show on ITV1, *Cheryl Cole's Night In*, was transmitted, and she enthused, 'I couldn't be happier that I have been asked to round off the year with my own show, working with some of my favourite artists.' Among the guests lined up were Rihanna, Will Young and Alexandra Burke – Cheryl's protégée who had won *The X-Factor* the previous year.

It was a success that was to be repeated when the 2009 series came to an end watched by more than 19 million viewers; and Cheryl's mentored act, Joe McElderry, was voted the winner – and he was effusive in his praise for her. The 18-year-old from South Shields said, 'I had the best mentor, especially for the fact that she was from the same place as me. It was really good having somebody like that to go and talk to. She was really supportive and helpful with the song choices, so it was really good. She told me to just enjoy it and don't believe your own hype. She said that a lot. Enjoy your singing, because the moment you start believing your own hype, you lose the focus of the competition and it kind of ruins it.

'She teaches performance skills, different hand movements that are more effective. And she'll come on to the stage and say, "Try this or try that" and it'll have more effect.'

Asked about his crush on Cheryl he replied, 'Oh, who doesn't fancy Cheryl Cole? Come on!'

He wasn't alone in his feelings for Cheryl. Prince Harry, an avid fan of the show, had been a VIP guest at the final and afterwards he told the young singer that he was 'so jealous that you got to spend weeks with Cheryl'.

For her part Cheryl, who had yet to commit for a third season of the show, said after her act's triumph, 'I would like a hat-trick. I'll give it a go.'

As Christmas 2009 drew near, there was yet more speculation over the state of Cheryl and Ashley's marriage, although she was spotted wearing her wedding ring on this occasion when she went to see Chelsea beat Portsmouth 2–1 at Stamford Bridge, leaving the ground in the passenger seat of Ashley's new Bentley.

Many interpreted the absence of her ring as being an indication that all was not well with the couple, but Cheryl had a much more down-to-earth explanation when she gave an interview to *Glamour* magazine in January 2010, in which she said the strain of gossip about her marriage had pushed Ashley to melting point.

She said, 'He broke down to me about it all. He called me from the garage and said: "I feel sick. I'm on the cover of every magazine because apparently I've made you cry."' She said that on occasions she didn't wear her ring as it clashed with the clothes she was wearing. 'Do people really think I'm going to have an argument and take my ring off? It was a fashion statement more than a marriage statement. As my wedding ring is yellow it doesn't go with everything.

'My family love Ashley but even people really close to me are starting to believe that there's a rift between us. Ashley is totally the opposite of how he is perceived. People have this idea that he is flash, ignorant and disloyal – the ugliest traits a husband could have. But he's not. He's never rude, he's never aggressive and will go out of his way to make other people happy. He's shy and he's cute, but there it is. God knows why I have been slapped with the fashionista tag. I still have days all the time when I feel sh***y or I have cellulite. But Ashley will tell me I am gorgeous and I will feel all right.'

Cheryl – who had been on a New Year break to South Africa with her mother; Ashley was busy with Chelsea at the time – also said the backlash from her fame almost felt like bullying at times: 'It's a strong word to use, but when you have people on Twitter saying, "Look at her fat hanging out," or "Look at her big nose," you feel people have forgotten you're a human being.'

That sunshine holiday in South Africa was a rare break for Cheryl. The commitments she and Ashley had made it difficult to escape for breaks, although in the summer the couple, with Chelsea defender Wayne Bridge and his girlfriend Vanessa Perroncel, had holidayed in the South of France.

Back in the UK, two stories emphasised the world Cheryl had come from and the one she now inhabited.

Ashley was been banned from driving for doing more

than 100mph in a 50mph zone after a speed gun recorded him driving his black Lamborghini Gallardo at 104mph.

Magistrates at Kingston, Surrey, imposed a four-month ban and £1,000 fine, although his legal team immediately launched an appeal. He was on the A3 in Kingston when he was clocked speeding. Though he denied the charge – he said he had been pursued by photographers at the time – he had been convicted at an earlier hearing.

The magistrates said, 'We have taken into account Mr Cole's clean licence; however, this was an incident of excessive speed, over twice the speed limit on the road, and these were exceptional circumstances, which we need to mark.' He was also ordered to pay a £15 victim surcharge and £300 costs to reflect his income and the seriousness of the offence. His defence barrister asked for 21 days to pay, which magistrates laughed at but granted.

Meanwhile, Cheryl's wayward brother Andrew was hit with a three-year driving ban. A court heard that he'd been caught in a car at three times the legal alcohol limit. Andrew was unable to produce a valid driving licence or insurance documents for the vehicle, a Peugeot 206, which he had allegedly been driving at 10mph with no lights at 4.30 in the morning. Before officers could approach the car, it was said, Andrew ran off towards nearby houses and hid in bushes, but homeowners raised the alarm. He pleaded guilty to driving with excess alcohol, having no insurance and driving otherwise in accordance with a licence at North Tyneside Magistrates' Court. The admissions meant he was automatically guilty of breaching his outstanding 36-week suspended prison sentence for common assault and possession of a pepper spray handed down in May the previous year.

A judge at Newcastle Crown Court subsequently said, 'You clearly have a number of personal problems that you need to attend to and I accept that this is a completely different type of offence from those which you were originally sentenced for.'

Judge Faulks spared him a prison term and instead amended the existing suspended sentence to include an 18-month supervision requirement and a 12-month drug-rehabilitation requirement.

He was also fined £100 and told he must attend a programme known as 'addressing substance-related offending' (ASRO). Tweedy had more than 80 previous convictions in total by this time.

These two cases were perfect illustrations of the lifestyles of Geordie lass Cheryl Tweedy and superstar Cheryl Cole. Perhaps it was this contrast and the manner in which she had moved from one world to the other that explained why so many people felt a genuine affection for her and were concerned about every problem she encountered. The next few weeks were to provide many more dramas for her and her legion of fans, and headlines even Cheryl had never experienced before.

12

BRITS ALL OVER?

Ironically it was almost Valentine's Day when the final scandals broke.

The rumourmongers had been working overtime on Cheryl and Ashley's marriage, the cynics were sneering at their lifestyle and the bookies were happy to take bets on when the couple would separate, but none of them could have predicted what was to happen next. Who could have?

It involved a topless model, raunchy photographs and suggestive text messages, in a scenario so bizarre that if invented would have been deemed too implausible for words.

It was 12 February 2010 when the *Sun* carried the story that many feel publicly signified the beginning of the end for the Golden Couple. Sonia Wild, a statuesque 28-year-old from Hull, had received snaps of Ashley stripped and 'in all his glory' on her mobile phone. She replied with naked videos of herself during hours of fairly explicit exchanges. It was an astonishing revelation.

Ashley admitted that the snaps had been taken by himself, reflected in a bathroom mirror, but he had just been 'larking about' while with the England World Cup squad when they were staying in a Hertfordshire hotel. And Ashley, who was out of the game with a broken ankle at the time the story broke, insisted he wasn't the man who sent her the pictures during hours of text sex.

The Chelsea player told the newspaper what they described as 'the amazing chain of events' that saw the explicit pictures end up on the model's mobile.

Ashley maintained that he had given the phone away to a pal because it still had some credit left on it, saying, 'I can't believe I gave a phone away that still had stuff in its memory. I thought I'd deleted it. It seems I was wrong as someone has used it to pretend to be me. I would laugh if my foot didn't hurt so much.' He was to claim that the pictures and messages were sent by someone pretending to be him.

A source close Ashley was quoted in the report as saying, 'Ashley's embarrassed about this. He was larking about in his room with his camera-phone before the match. He was in all his glory. He took the images on an unregistered pay-as-you-go phone, then didn't manage to delete them when he gave it away to a mate. To say he's horrified to discover the pictures were sent to a model is an understatement.'

Ashley said he had been using the unregistered mobile

because he was 'between phones' and subsequently gave it to a friend, named in the newspaper as Jay Wynters. Then, unknown to the soccer star, Wynters passed it on to a friend, who found the images and decided to hoodwink Wild by sending them to her.

Ashley was shirtless in one of the pictures and it had the caption 'I look so ugly'. Others were 'too rude to print in a family newspaper', the *Sun* said.

Single mother-of-two Sonia, who had posed for lads' mags in the past, was quoted as saying, 'At first I didn't believe I was actually in touch with Ashley Cole. But next thing I knew I received a picture of him lying in bed on my phone.

'I recognised him straight away from the pictures I'd seen of him with his wife Cheryl but couldn't resist having a bit of fun. It was exciting getting a picture of a soccer star.

'I'd had a few glasses of wine and before long the texts got hotter and hotter until we began exchanging sexy images on our phones. Whoever it was sent one full frontal one of his muscly torso. He was posing in front of what looked like a posh hotel's bathroom mirror. The texting and picture messaging went on for hours.

'I sent back video footage recorded on my phone of myself naked and doing sexy things for him. At the time it was a laugh and a bit of a thrill for me.'

The telephone encounter, according to her, came on 9 June the previous year, the day before her birthday and also the night prior to England's beating Andorra 6–0 in a crucial World Cup qualifying clash.

Ashley, who played in the game, had stayed at the five-star Grove in Kings Langley, Hertfordshire, the night before the Wembley match. Wild's phone bill shows she sent 28 messages back to the phone. The next morning she recorded four more sexy pictures of herself in the bath and sent one to the unregistered mobile at 10.34am.

She sent a total of six texts to the phone on 10 June up until 6.09pm – approximately two hours before the match kicked off. She said she carried on getting flirty texts from whoever had the phone for more than a month until, in June, the texter said he would be 'uncontactable' for a while.

Sonia said she received more texts begging her to fix a meeting. She added, 'The person who kept texting asked me to go and meet him in London. But I'd been drunk when we had text sex and felt bad about actually meeting him. The texting was just a bit of a laugh on my side, but he was obviously serious and I eventually had to tell him, "No way."

'He kept telling me how gorgeous I was and that we had to meet up – but I honestly wasn't interested in seeing him. I played him along but there was no way I was ever going to meet him in the flesh. I had no idea it wasn't Ashley Cole.'

During the texting, Sonia said several messages also begged her to join the sender in America.

The texts began, she said, after she had become friendly online with Cole's pal Jay Wynters. She said, 'I have never met Jay in person. But he had a picture of himself on his profile with Ashley Cole and another man, who I think is also an England footballer.

'He said he had a friend who wanted to get in touch and asked if he could pass on my number. I asked who it was and he said it was the man with him in his profile picture. Now I know that was a lie,' she was quoted as saying.

The day the story broke, Cheryl, in the front of a chauffer-driven car, collected Ashley from the hospital in St John's Wood where he had been treated for his broken ankle. Several newspapers reported that Victoria Beckham had contacted Cheryl to offer her comfort over the strain the reports had placed her under.

But that weekend there were more disclosures from Sonia Wild that told a different story. This time she was quoted at length in the *Sunday Mirror* and gave more details of what went on between her and the person sending her messages, saying, 'If that wasn't Ashley Cole, then I'm a nun. I've said all along that it was Ashley who was doing all the running, sending me pictures of himself, texting and phoning me.

'I've listened to Ashley's softly spoken voice in interviews on TV and it was unmistakably him.'

She told the paper's reporter, 'Ashley's denying that it was him who sent me the pictures. But maybe he also needs to ask this – why would another man go around texting me pictures of Ashley's private parts?' She said her first conversation came two hours before the kick-off against Andorra after they had been messaging each other all day.

She maintained he called her at least three more times

over the next four weeks. In one of the calls, she said he asked her to join in him in America. He also asked if she would like to meet in London or Hull when Chelsea were next playing there. But each time she turned down his offers.

'I told him sending sexy texts and pictures was one thing, but meeting up was another,' she said. 'I couldn't believe it when he asked me to fly out to America. He said he could organise a flight and hotel, but that it would have to be in another name.'

Sonia, who had two daughters aged 11 and 9, added, 'I was flattered. I think any girl would be. Especially when he is so high-profile and was clearly happy to risk being found out. I said, "thanks but no thanks", and just said my life was too busy with work and my kids,' she told the paper.

She said the astonishing chain of events began when she received a message on the social networking site MySpace from 'a mutual friend, Jay Wynters.' The party promoter had been badgering her for years to go to VIP club nights attended by footballers. She said that Wynters asked if he could pass on her number to a friend who wanted to contact her, and he said it was one of the men with him in his profile pictures, Ashley Cole or fellow England international Shaun Wright-Phillips.

'I received a text from a number I didn't recognise on the afternoon of June 9, which said "Hi Sonia, it's Jay's friend."

'I sent back a message saying, "Is it Shaun Wright-Phillips?" The text came back "No" – so I asked him to send a picture to prove who he was,' the *Sunday Mirror* continued.

She was immediately sent a picture of Ashley reclining in a king-size bed and she recognised it straight away. 'I recognised him immediately and couldn't believe it. It was so exciting to get the photo of him. He'd obviously checked me out on MySpace because he kept saying how sexy I was and what a fantastic body I had,' she told the paper.

For hours they exchanged sexy text messages and naked images of each other, she said, and the next morning she sent a picture of herself naked in the bath. Later that day she was called by Ashley, she added. 'I model for a living, I'm very good at turning men on. It was a laugh and a great story to tell my friends. I even forwarded the shots of him to my mum.'

Sonia said she was called later the following day. 'He never said, "It's Ashley" – he was always careful never to do that, the four times that he and I spoke on the phone he just said, "Hi" or, "Hi, babe, it's me." '

She said he asked to meet up in London but she said she could not do that, as she had to look after her daughters. She had no intention of starting an affair, she said, but she 'didn't want to bruise his ego'.

Her mother Michelle telephoned her on 15 June to say she'd spotted pictures of Ashley and Cheryl flying off to the South of France for a holiday with friends, the report said.

'When I looked at the pictures of Ashley at the airport with Cheryl I recognised the watch he was wearing from the text pictures he'd sent me,' said Sonia. 'I didn't expect to hear from him again, but a few days later he texted me.

It was from the same mobile phone, because his name came up. That conversation was very brief.'

In July she says it was suggested that she go to America and it was then that she said that texting was one thing but meeting up was another. She had only a couple more text messages after that.

She concluded by telling the paper, 'There has never been any doubt in my mind that the calls, texts, pictures were 100 per cent all from Ashley. I have a successful career as a model and I would never want to jeopardise that. I've no reason to lie.'

A story of this nature would have been sensational at any time, but, coming hard on the heels of Ashley's England and Chelsea teammate John Terry being stripped of the England captaincy over his relationship with Wayne Bridge's former girlfriend Vanessa Perroncel, it had even greater impact.

The disclosures also coincided with the publication of an interview Cheryl had given to *Hello!* in which she said, 'I've never defended him and I don't want to go into this subject. But my message is still the same. If it's worth fighting for then fight. And, in the case of me and my husband, it's worth it.

'We love each other. Of course, sometimes when things aren't going very well, you've got to work on your relationship. Sometimes one of you makes a mistake, sometimes the other.

'Well, let's not kid ourselves. We're not at primary school any more. Let's just say that during the first six to twelve months everything is always great. You're totally in love and everything works by itself. Then, at some point, everyday life takes over again. I think that's normal.'

It couldn't get much worse for Cheryl – or could it?

The next day the *Sun* had fresh revelations about calls from Ashley's phone, this time to blonde secretary Vicki Gough, who it did not initially name but whose identity was soon to become public knowledge.

The paper didn't pull any punches when it said, 'Shameless Ashley Cole is today exposed as a liar and a sex text cheat after X-rated messages and photos of him were found on *another* blonde's mobile phone.

'The England footie ace, 29, wed to *X Factor* star Cheryl sent the secretary hundreds of lurid texts. Cole's new shame emerged just days after he explained away nude photos of himself found on a topless model's mobile.

'Cole last week insisted he had been "larking about" when he took explicit snaps of himself on a pay-as-you-go mobile while "between phones".

'The Chelsea defender said the pictures were sent to glamour girl Sonia Wild after he gave the temporary mobile to a friend, who passed it to another pal.'

The story continued, 'But that explanation is today exposed as a lie as the *Sun* reveals another woman received virtually *identical* pictures of Cole and more than 300 text messages – sent from the *same* phone nine months earlier.'

The tabloid reported that some of the pictures showed Ashley in just a pair of white pants and others were 'too obscene to mention'.

The woman received hundreds of texts over a two-month period, most of which were sent while Cheryl had been working as a judge on *The X-Factor*. During the very first text session, on 4 October 2008, he wrote, 'I beg u keep this between us x.' Minutes later he added, 'Please delete all texts ill [I'll] have no balls left.'

As the two exchanged ever more explicit messages, he again stressed the need for secrecy on 9 October, when he sent a text that read, 'we both have things 2 lose i do trust u alot. And i would never show any1.'

The longest barrage – a total of 57 messages – was sent on the weekend of 25 and 26 October 2008. Minutes before sending a picture of his private parts at 3.32am on 26 October, Cole joked, 'No its not big. Ur make me laugh. X,' the *Sun* reported.

The next day, Cole sent a message saying, 'Hello how r u 2day recovered from our text a thon. Ha x.'

The woman also told the newspaper that on two occasions she was sneaked into the team hotel for sex with him before away games.

The first time, he sent her texts telling her to go to a room booked under the name of a club official, and, on the second, a team aide in a tracksuit collected her from the hotel lobby and silently led her to the player's room.

Once she was inside, the paper said, he turned up the volume and said 'JT [John Terry] is next door – I don't want him to hear us.'

The blonde said, 'Ashley begged me to come to his hotel for sex, but it was like a military operation getting into the room. On both occasions I had to smuggle in a bottle of rosé wine for us to drink in bed because he wasn't supposed to drink before games. He was petrified of getting caught by his wife *and* by Chelsea, but he just couldn't stop himself taking crazy risks,' the *Sun* said.

After a long period of illicit messaging, the pair finally met the night before Chelsea's match at Hull on 29 October 2008. The woman described in detail how she had always fancied Ashley and drove to Hull after work and went to the Forest Pines Hotel in north Lincolnshire. She was worried that it might not be Ashley who would meet her and that it would be 'some dodgy bloke', but eventually he came to a room that he had arranged for her to stay in

The secretary told how she and Cole watched two uninspiring science-fiction films before having sex. She added, 'It wasn't raunchy stuff, more like relationship sex. The whole thing was surreal. I thought this toned athlete with a reputation as a ladies' man would be throwing me all over the bed. But it was quite the opposite.'

After she returned home he continued sending lewd texts and asking her to send him nude pictures of herself. One message read, 'can i have 1 more of ur tits,' the *Sun* said.

The second liaison was on Friday, 14 November 2008, the night before Chelsea played at West Bromwich Albion, and again they were intimate. She said, 'He never once mentioned Cheryl's name. The papers at the time were saying he and Cheryl were thinking about starting a family, but he skirted round that and didn't seem keen – he said kids would change your life so much.'

They never met again and their text messages ended on 5 December 2008.

The *Sun* reported that day that spokesmen for Ashley and Chelsea both declined to comment. A few days after the story appeared, the woman was identified first on fan websites and then in local and national newspapers as Vicki Gough, a 31-year-old secretary at Liverpool FC. Soon afterwards she left the club 'by mutual consent'.

The day the story appeared of Gough's fling with Ashley, Cheryl had to perform at the Brits Awards, and, in front of a star-studded audience, she bravely made it through an energetic rendition of her hit single with a wink and a smile. She had cancelled all her promotion around the event but gave a show-stopping performance.

The *Daily Mail*'s Jan Moir , under the heading AND THE AWARD FOR SLEAZIEST HUSBAND GOES TO ... MRS COLE, wrote:

Brava Cheryl! There she stood in the spotlight, the celebrated wronged wife, the nation's favourite munchkin martyr, the fairytale sweetheart undone by her very own big, bad wolf. Never mind her constant proclamations of unity and the fact that she has Mrs Cole tattooed in cursive script across the back of her neck. Her Premier league footballer husband's sex texts, then subsequent sex trysts with a fruity secretary – and his narcissistic penchant for photographing himself naked – have all exposed his contempt for her. Not to mention his own plutonium grade selfishness and max strength stupidity.

No wonder that underneath a pair of sooty fake lashes, Cheryl's big, brown Coca-Cola eyes softly fizzed with puzzled hurt. 'We've got to fight, fight for this love,' she sang, reprising the chorus of her hit solo single. What a mocking, hollow refrain that now sounds, doesn't it? ...

'Yet the one man who matters treats her like common or garden dirt; what did Cheryl ever do to deserve Ashley Cole? And why has this happened to her?

Even Ashley's father, factory worker Ron Callender, joined the criticism. 'This is as though Ashley is asking for Cheryl to divorce him. I can't say I'd blame her if she did. Cheryl has been shamed by what Ashley has done,' he said. 'People may be nice to her face because she's a famous singer, but they will be looking at her and thinking she's a mug for sticking by him after all he's done.'

Callender separated from Ashley's mother when his son was three, but always kept in touch. Speaking from Melbourne, Australia, he said, 'Even though he's my son, I can't condone what he's done. His excuse to Cheryl last time when he had a one-night stand with another woman was that he was so drunk he didn't know what he was doing. Well he can't have been drunk again. That's a pathetic excuse.'

He said, 'Ashley was brought up by his mum, my ex-partner Susan, to respect women, not send naked pictures of himself in a state of arousal to girls he doesn't even know. His mother will be mortified by his behaviour.

'Susan was the driving force behind his soccer career. He owes her everything. Ashley loves his mum. He's a real mummy's boy, so I'm baffled by his behaviour. I don't understand how he can treat women this way.'

Ron, who had followed his son's career and spoke regularly to him on the phone, said, 'I have been proud to watch Ashley rise through the football ranks with Arsenal, Chelsea and England. My proudest moment was being in the crowd to see him play for England against Brazil in the World Cup in 2002.

'I hope they stay together. But Ashley has to realise he's not a silly teenager any more. He's a man of 29, married to the most beautiful girl, who he says he loves, and his wife is talking about quitting work to have a baby.'

The day after the Brits, Cheryl wore giant sunglasses and appeared deep in thought as she prepared to leave London's Heathrow Airport to continue with her scheduled week-long writing and recording trip to Los Angeles. A spokesman for her said, 'Cheryl is going to America for writing and recording sessions. This is a session that was scheduled last month. She is away for a week. We have no further comment to make.'

The absence of her wedding ring at the Brits and when flying out to LA was noted – and not just by the press. The next day Ashley called the police at 4.30am saying, 'Please come quick. Someone's trying to break in,' as a window was forced at the couple's £4 million mansion. Police were convinced the raiders were after Cheryl's two diamond bands: the £150,000 heart-shaped diamond wedding ring and another, square-cut, dazzler worth £160,000. Police worked on the theory that the raiders decided she had left the wedding rings at home in Surrey and they would be easy pickings and did not expect Ashley to be there.

A senior police source said, 'It cannot be coincidence that people attempt to break into the family home when both of them are due to be out of the UK. And it happens when there's been widespread publicity that Mrs Cole is not wearing her wedding ring.'

The saga over Ashley's womanising had now reached a stage where, when the couple's marriage was analysed in print, it was necessary to have a brief 'history' of the women linked with him in order that readers did not get too confused. It invariably began by recalling Aimee Walton, the hairdresser who had surfaced some time earlier, and then mentioned Sonia Wild and Vicki Gough. Soon there were more names to add to the list in what had become an astonishing week. The revelations about Ashley seemed to be never-ending. It came as no surprise that, with the weekend reports detailing more claims from women about Ashley's behaviour, there were stories that Cheryl had texted him from Los Angeles. The message was said to be a simple one: a friend of the singer was quoted as saying, 'Cheryl has decided enough is enough and she is going to divorce him. She has told Ashley to get out of the family home because she does not wish to see him. She has no desire to hear any more excuses or explanations.'

The text, it was reported, simply said, 'Move out. It's over.'

Cheryl returned from a week-long trip to the States on Tuesday, 23 February. Dressed in black and hidden behind large black sunglasses and a trilby hat and flanked by two police officers, she was ushered through a side exit in the arrivals lounge. She headed for her home in a Mercedes at the same time as Ashley left for the South of France for specialist treatment on his injured ankle.

While she was in California, Cheryl's every move was monitored by the press and she had been photographed wearing an 'I Left my Heart in Beverly Hills' T-shirt. She had been escorted by American dancer Derek Hough, whom she met when she recorded the album *3 Words*. Hough, who appeared in *Dancing with the Stars*, the US version of *Strictly Come Dancing*, co-starred in Cole's video for her single 'Parachute'. Hough, who honed his moves as a dancer in West End shows, clicked with Cheryl when he partnered her on ITV1's *A Night in With Cheryl Cole* two months earlier. He also enjoyed a steamy ballroom dance with her in 'Parachute'. Cheryl had declared in an interview for MTV, 'I absolutely love Derek's work, so it's a pleasure to be working with him. He's a sweetheart.' And Derek posted on Twitter, 'Just finished rehearsal with Cheryl Cole. She's great to work with.'

Although a spokesperson for the star refused to comment on the suggestion that she had texted Ashley to leave the marital home, soon the news that everyone had been predicting became official. It was 28 words long and lasted just three sentences. It said: 'Cheryl Cole is separating from her husband Ashley Cole. Cheryl asks the media to respect her privacy during this difficult time. We have no further comment to make.'

So that was it. After three and a half years of marriage, it had all come down to this. Even though there had been countless voices, some knowledgeable some pure guesswork, saying that this end was bound to happen in the course of time, it seemed hard to accept that the marriage was now on the rocks.

A galaxy of 'friends', 'sources', 'pals' and 'insiders' came forth to give their views on the breakdown. The universal opinion, certainly among those who had written at length about the strains on the marriage, was that its end was inevitable and Ashley was the villain of the piece. Although it was claimed that he desperately tried to speak to her in Los Angeles, and even offered to attend rehab or counselling in order that she stay, she did not want to even take his calls. The continuing revelations had been too much for Cheryl to take, everyone said, and there were only so many times that Ashley could be forgiven.

Those fighting his corner, seeking some explanation for his behaviour, came up with answers ranging from the fact that too many young women targeted wealthy young footballers such as Ashley, to the close relationship Cheryl had with her mother Joan. Whatever the truth of the matter, one thing was for certain. It was all over, the dream marriage of the Golden Couple – the Nation's Sweetheart and 'Ashley' Cole – had ceased to be.

Cheryl stayed indoors at their home; Ashley, too, refused to divulge any information. At the clinic where he was being treated in Capbreton, a seaside town near Biarritz, he dodged all questions, saying, 'I just can't talk about that.' Ashley was with teammate Michael Essien and physio Thierry Laurent, and the England star tried to hide behind an exercise machine. Wearing a supportive sandal on his injured foot, he hobbled away on crutches after refusing to answer any questions.

Ashley flew home on 13 March to see Cheryl, the first time the two had met in over three weeks since the stories about him and the string of women had emerged. The meeting lasted just under an hour and the matters to be discussed were dividing their wealth – there had been no prenup signed prior to their wedding – and even the fate of their pet Chihuahuas, Buster and Coco.

He had flown in from Biarritz in Chelsea owner Roman Abramovich's white private jet. From a Surrey airport he was then driven in a limo straight to his mansion in the county, arriving at 7pm. He hid in the back seat to try to avoid being seen.

Cheryl was waiting inside. She had earlier cancelled an appearance on *Friday Night with Jonathan Ross* and a performance on Radio 1 due to bronchitis. But she did appear on *Sport Relief* on the BBC at the end of March, laughing at a spoof of her act by comedian Rufus Hound, and then earning a massive round of applause and affection for her performance of 'Parachute'.

Support for Cheryl had been widespread, perhaps best

summed up by comments even from the woman who, at first mistaken glance, might have been thought to have an axe to grind with her. Sharon Osbourne, had been replaced by Cheryl on *X-Factor*.

The couple shared a private box at a Lady Gaga concert at the O2 arena soon after the separation was announced. 'She looked divine, not distressed. She was really, really OK. Look, she can't be doing that badly if she's out there enjoying herself. Absolutely good luck to her,' Osbourne said. 'She's a young woman, blessed with talent and beauty, she's got it all going for her. She was talking about Los Angeles – she's keen to get back there.

'I love strong, independent women. She's got a great career, she's sassy and approachable. She'll do brilliantly in America – they'll love her. How could you not? Look, she's 26, she's got no kids and she made a mistake. Time to move on. We all get one love of our life who hurts us. It's not usually the one we walk down the aisle with. Cheryl was 23 when she married Ashley. I mean, come on, they were kids. You make a great-looking couple and at that age you think it's the best thing ever. Cheryl's a self-made woman and should be proud of herself. And she's surrounded by people who love her.

'How many men must be rubbing their hands now? She's going to need a bodyguard to keep them all away.'

Wise words from Mrs Ozzy Osbourne and hope for a future for both Cheryl and Ashley – whatever it holds.